Springer Series on

ADULTHOOD and AGING

Series Editors: Lissy F. Jarvik, M.D., Ph.D.,
    and Bernard D. Starr, Ph.D.

Advisory Board: Paul B. Baltes, Ph.D., Jack Botwinick, Ph.D.,
    Carl Eisdorfer, M.D., Ph.D., Robert Kastenbaum, Ph.D.,
    Neil G. McCluskey, Ph.D., K. Warner Schaie, Ph.D.,
    and Nathan W. Shock, Ph.D.

ADULT DAY CARE
Community Work with the Elderly

Philip G. Weiler
Eloise Rathbone-McCuan

with contributions by
Annette Castle & Larry Pickard

SPRINGER PUBLISHING COMPANY
New York

Springer Publishing Company, Inc.
200 Park Avenue South
New York, N.Y. 10003

362. 6

Wei

78 79 80 81 82 / 10 9 8 7 6 5 4 3 2 1

Library of Congress Cataloging in Publication Data

Weiler, Philip G
  Adult day care.

  (Springer series on adulthood and aging)
  Includes bibliographies.
  1. Community health services for the aged. 2. Social
work with the aged. I. Rathbone-McCuan, Eloise, joint
author. II. Title. III. Series.
RA564.8.W44   362.6'3   77-17593
ISBN 0-8261-2270-1
ISBN 0-8261-2271-X pbk.

Printed in the United States of America

To all of those who have come so appreciatively as participants to the Center for Creative Living, and in memory of Arthur and Max, who symbolized so much of what this book is intended to convey.

Contents

Contents

Contents

Foreword

Since 1900, life expectancy has increased steadily from 47.3 years to 72.4 years in 1975. In 1900, 3.1 million Americans—only four percent of the population—were 65 years old or more. By 1976, when our population was 214 million, 12.4 percent were older than 65. Now, more than 1.6 million of these elderly Americans are confined to long-term care facilities. Given the size of the group in need of care, alternatives to institutionalization are essential.

Each patient brings medical, psychological, social, and family problems to his physician, who must evaluate them carefully and determine treatment. Alternatives to institutionalization should be prescribed specifically by the physician in the same manner in which he prescribes digitalis or penicillin.

In the mid-1960s, professionals in the field of aging began to look upon geriatric day care centers as an innovative approach to the delivery of quality services to the elderly. Day care centers were first established as noninstitutional therapeutic environments for psychogeriatric patients. Somewhat later, the concept was expanded to meet the health and social needs of the functionally disabled.

This book is designed for health professionals and others concerned about the problems and issues associated with developing alternative forms of long-term care. The book addresses itself to the difficulties that are encountered in planning services and in the practical and relevant problems of administration in day care operations.

In the United States, day care is clearly a new frontier in health care and social change. This book should be extremely valuable to the reader as an introduction to this evolving concept.

WILLIAM REICHEL, M.D.
Franklin Square Hospital
Baltimore, Maryland

Contributors

Philip G. Weiler is Commissioner of Health for the Lexington-Fayette County Health Department and Professor and Chairman of the Department of Community Medicine at the University of Kentucky Medical School. In addition, he serves as medical consultant to the Department of Health, Education and Welfare and as a consultant to private industry. Dr. Weiler, Past President of both the Kentucky Public Health Association and the Kentucky Association of Public Health Physicians, received his B.S. from Loyola University, his M.D. from Tulane University, and his M.P.H. and M.P.A. from Harvard University. He is the author and coauthor of numerous articles and papers in the fields of health manpower, financing, organization, and health care for the aged.

Eloise Rathbone-McCuan is Assistant Professor of Social Work at Washington University, St. Louis. Dr. Rathbone-McCuan, former Director of the Levindale Geriatric Research Center, received her B.S. from the University of Kentucky and her M.S.W. and Ph.D. degrees from the University of Pittsburgh. An active member of the Gerontological Society and the American Geriatrics Society, she has authored and coauthored various articles in the field of geriatrics and day care.

Annette Castle is currently Director of Community Health Services, Lexington-Fayette County Health Department. Her nursing experience has included involvement in the development of Lexington's adult day health care centers, and she has served as the nurse member of a research and assessment team investigating alternatives in long term care for medicare recipients over 65 years. Ms. Castle was the major contributor for chapters 5 and 7 of this volume.

Paul K. H. Kim, Assistant Professor at the University of Kentucky College of Social Professions, received his B.S.W. degree from the Korea School of Social Work in Seoul, his M.S.W. from San Diego State University, and his D.S.W. from Tulane University. Dr. Kim was involved in the development of chapter 11.

Larry S. Pickard is presently the Director of Long Term Care at the Lexington-Fayette County Health Department. He completed his undergraduate studies at the University of Iowa and received his M.S.W. degree from the University of Kentucky, College of Social Professions. At the Lexington-Fayette County Health Department, he has been directly involved with the development, evaluation, and administration of two adult day care centers. Previously, he had clinical experience in psychiatric settings for geriatric clients. Mr. Pickard was a major contributor to chapters 4 and 8.

William G. Weissert is a health services research fellow at the National Center for Health Services Research, U.S. Public Health Service, and Adjunct Associate Professor of Political Science at George Washington University. He holds a B.S. from Portland State University, an M.S. from Northwestern University, and a Ph.D. from Claremont Graduate School. Dr. Weissert was the major contributor for chapter 3.

ADULT DAY CARE
Community Work with the Elderly

1

Day Care as a Long-Term Care Alternative

Introduction and Background

There is growing nationwide interest in a broad human-services movement to search for noninstitutional long-term care alternatives. This interest is partially prompted by the human and financial consequences of overreliance on institutional care. Adult day care is one of the service programs being developed as a long-term care alternative to increase the options available to the impaired elderly and thereby improve their quality of life.

This book discusses the problems and issues associated with emerging forms of long-term care. It specifically addresses the planning, development, and delivery of day care services within the conceptual framework of long-term care.

The chapters have been organized to cover a wide range of issues to provide information useful to those who are encountering many of the difficulties of planning, implementing, and evaluating day care centers for the elderly.

An overview of the problem identifies the major social and health aspects of long-term care and develops a supportive argument for day care center service. The historical development of centers in northern Europe and the United States is examined and the current status of these services is used as a guideline for understanding present and future service trends. The day care services of the Urban County Health Department in Lexington, Kentucky, and the Levindale Hebrew Geriatric Center and Hospital in Baltimore, Maryland, and the varied operational components of these centers illustrate the issues involved in the day care movement. Some of the most problematic aspects of service are explored: specialized roles and services provided by medicine, nursing, and social work staff; the role of the family in the day care setting; methods and techniques for intake and discharge; the financial and administrative aspects of day care operations. A final section is devoted to program evaluation and discusses recommendations for future policy formulation.

The authors recognize that this book is neither the first nor the final work on adult day care; it is an initial effort to approach the subject comprehensively and to provide a foundation for more knowledge.

Long-Term Care Needs

One of the most tragic commentaries on our times is the accusation that we have buried the aged alive in their homes, in institutions, in hospitals.[1] The litany of abuses and problems in meeting the human service needs of the aged is long and well publicized in the press, congressional reports, and books. The present system is insensitive, inadequate, and excessively harsh. It attempts to reduce the needs of the elderly to the lowest common denominator—institutional care.

Although concern about the plight of the elderly has been developing for decades, it seems that the problems of the aged are neither a strong political issue nor very visible until scandals are exposed. For example, little has been done to implement recommendations of the White House Conference on Aging from 1971,[2] the National Council of Senior Citizens,[3] or other professional groups.

New problems increase the pressure for action now. One is a "population explosion"; people aged 65 and older currently make up more than ten percent of the population, and they are the fastest growing minority, expected to double in size by the year 2050. Another reason is financial. The elderly account for one-fourth of the nation's health-care expenditure and one-fourth of all drugs used.

They are the major users of institutional beds, accounting for twice the number of bed-days as the rest of the population.[4]

The costs of providing long-term care for the elderly are escalating rapidly and, despite substantial federal investment, are an increasing burden for states. It is estimated that $11.5 billion in federal, state, and local funds were spent in fiscal year 1974 on long-term care.[5]

However, the most serious reason for action is the inability of the present system to cope with needs of the elderly. With two million people in long-term care facilities, including over five percent of all persons aged 65 and older, the problem is worsening. With the present system, one out of five senior citizens can expect to spend some time in a nursing home during his lifetime.[6]

The current crucial public policy decisions center on the problems of delivering long-term care. Long-term care refers to the external support systems needed by the aged to maintain life at a satisfactory level of quality, whether in community-based facilities, at home, or in institutions. This includes medical, economic, and/or social service help. Because the elderly require support in all these areas, it is obvious that long-term care should not be based solely on medical needs. Aside from these limitations, however, the medical approach has another disadvantage in that costs tend to escalate without any necessary relation to quality. One reason for such escalation is the increasing sophistication—and cost—of medical technology. Concomitantly, personnel become increasingly restricted to highly trained, licensed professionals who command high salaries. Another reason for rising costs with a medical approach has been the proliferation of expensive (and sometimes unnecessary) testing administered as a matter of routine. Called "defensive medicine," such testing is intended to protect those administering care against malpractice suits.

The problems of long-term care are broad and complex not only because they involve medical, social, economic, ethical, and political questions, but also because programs and policies are fragmented. Currently there are at least half a dozen categorical and uncoordinated programs at different levels of government that were created independently and funded to deal with specific needs of the aged. Facilities have developed to parallel financing mechanisms, and there is little understanding on the part of the public of the differences in client populations, service needs, and services provided in different facilities. People are often forced to choose a method of care without considering any of the alternatives because of lack of knowledge, inaccessibility of care, or financing arrangements. Although the financing maze for institutional care is confusing and plagued with gaps, the picture for noninstitutional care and alternative care is even more complex.

A Framework for Long-Term Care

Traditionally, long-term care has been defined as a health service, with secondary consideration given to the social care element. The reverse is seldom the case. There are two reasons for this: First, most facilities have no stated long-range goals and objectives; rather, they are geared to intervention in acute problems. Second, as a result of health-oriented reimbursement policies, authorization for experimentation such as geriatric day care centers as an alternative to institutionalization is legislated as health care. Therefore, experimentation is markedly limited and results in numerous variations on old themes rather than in timely new approaches. The grandiloquent and sometimes heated exchanges between medical and nonmedical practitioners rarely lead to adequate service integration, but this essential issue must be faced.

We propose a new philosophic framework that deemphasizes a series of discrete stages in the aging process and emphasizes the diversity of the aged population. This framework is based not on myths or prejudices about aging but on the realities.[7] A recent survey on attitudes toward the aged has provided much insight into these realities.[8] Equal weight must be given to biomedical, psychological, socioeconomic, and sociocultural needs. Care of the elderly must extend over an indefinite period of time; it requires flexible and diverse supports to provide a broad range of community services that enable the elderly to remain in their homes for as long as possible with freedom to exercise individual initiative.

In this framework the care continuum is defined as services and people and the interaction between them. The services should have the following characteristics:[9]

1. Supports should be continuous or for specific time intervals that extend beyond the acute problem.

2. Access should be flexible and promptly available.

3. Mechanisms should exist to assess individual need at the community level.

4. The environmental setting should encourage the individual to make use of his functional strengths.

5. There should be follow-up on the continuing needs of the individual.

6. There should be adequate facilities.

7. Services should be appropriate to the target population.

8. Services should vary in their degree of complexity and avoid duplication of resources.

The archaic practice of trying to fit individuals into prepackaged service settings leads to a morass of definitions of facilities and levels of care. This fragmentation could go on indefinitely. The level of care should be based solely on the individual and not on the setting, making it possible to provide a continuum of care tailored to each individual's changing needs. This care continuum would insure flexibility within a single service and among services. People would be able to move freely between settings without jeopardizing the overall quality of their care; indeed, referral would be part of the plan to meet their needs. Services would be provided in appropriate settings: institutional, congregate living arrangement, private home, or the person's own home.

To assure that the services meet individual needs, a method of assessment must be established. This mechanism should provide recommendations for services, referrals, and consumer feedback. Community-based counselors, perhaps older citizens themselves, could act as facilitators and "brokers" of service to follow up on recommendations and complaints. As assessment team composed of medical and social work professionals would develop specific care plans for each individual. Mechanisms for manipulating funding sources would be provided through community long-term care coordinating agencies such as are being developed in Wisconsin,[10] Connecticut (triage program),[11] New York,[12] and other states.

Day Care as a Long-Term Care Service

During the past four years, the geriatric day care center has become increasingly important to policy makers, service providers, and researchers concerned with the demonstration and evaluation of these concepts. There has been an attempt to move in the direction of a rational plan for introducing the concept in the United States. At the federal government level, three particular agencies within the Department of Health, Education, and Welfare have assumed major leadership roles: the National Center for Health Services Research, Division of Long-Term Care; the Administration on Aging, Office of Human Development; and the Medical Services Administration, Division of Long-Term Care, Social Rehabilitation Services. Even prior to the passage of P.L. 92–603 (Social Security Amendments of 1972), key individuals within these agencies were farsighted enough to work toward instituting a plan for select field experiments that would test the effectiveness and cost of geriatric day care center services. In addition, many other state and local governmental officials have worked actively to develop guidelines that could structure the expansion of day care services at the local level and eventually lead to the passage of legislation needed to support the delivery of these services nationally as part of the spectrum of health-social services for the aged.

Geriatric day care is a broad concept that applies to any service provided during the day. It encompasses many types of services ranging from home care to day hospital. It has been implemented for nutritional, recreational, social, and health programs, and is an increasingly popular means of providing services to older people.

Many taxonomies have been proposed for day care services.[13] While these are helpful conceptually, they should not prevent flexibility for participants' needs and adaptability to local community needs. We prefer to break down the major service modalities concerned with day care centers as shown in Table 1.1.

Day care is a unique service modality because it can meet the long-term needs of those seeking service while also taking into account individual differences. It differs from outpatient services and senior centers in several important aspects: services are tailored spe-

Table 1.1   Geriatric Day Services

Modality	Major Service Objective	Type of Client	Service Setting
Day hospital	To provide daily medical care and supervision to help the individual regain an optimal level of health following an acute illness	Individual is in active phase of recovering from an acute illness, no longer requiring intense medical intervention on a periodic basis	Extended care facility or hospital
Social/ health center	To provide health care resources when required to chronically impaired individuals	Individual has chronic physical illness or disabilities; condition does not require daily medical intervention but does require nursing and other health supports	Long-term care institution or free-standing center
Psycho-social center	To provide a protective or transitional environment that assists the individual in dealing with multiple problems of daily coping	Individual has a history of psychiatric disorder; could reactivate and/or suffer from mental deterioration (organic or functional) that places him in danger if he is not closely supervised	Psychiatric institution or free-standing center
Social center	To provide appropriate socialization services	Individual's social functioning has regressed to the point where, without formal, organized social stimuli, overall capacity for independent functioning would not be possible	Specialized senior citizen center

cifically for each participant; each service has a therapeutic objective —prevention, maintenance, or rehabilitation; each day is planned for each individual and activities are not chosen at random by the participant (as is the case in many senior centers).

Among the candidates for day care are people who are living alone and cannot completely care for themselves, people who are living with others who need relief from the total responsibility of their care, and people discharged from an institutional setting. They require services oriented to prevention of illness; maintenance, rehabilitation, and restoration of health; and social contacts to overcome the isolation associated with illness and disability.

Day care service is delivered on three levels: individual, center, and the broader care continuum. It is from these levels that the day care center delivery system will be analyzed in the following chapters. The levels provide independent but related perspectives that are useful in the planning, implementation, and evaluation of day care centers. No perspective is better or worse; they are applied according to professional orientation and special uses concerning day care.

The individual perspective stresses the participant's experiences and permits consideration of his or her position in relation to personal care, planning, service impact, and staff and family interactions. For example, most day care centers designate socialization as one major service goal. However, since socialization involves an individual social interaction through social roles influenced by other people, one must assume an individual perspective to evaluate the experience.

The center perspective encompasses the day care center as a whole and allows for consideration of the quality and quantity of service. It emphasizes administrative and policy issues that are important to all day care center operations. For example, some day care centers have been established to provide an alternative to long-term institutional care, and cost-effectiveness is a major concern. To determine cost-effectiveness, one must consider the entire service operation.

The care continuum perspective approaches day care as part of a larger array of services and emphasizes planning, coordination, and community resources. For example, to determine if a center is required for a particular at-risk group, one must review the current array of a community's long-term care services to avoid duplication and to anticipate the possible links between the center and the other services. Successful planning also requires an examination of what groups currently are and are not being served.

Notes

1. Robert N. Butler, *Why Survive? Being Old in America* (New York: Harper and Row, 1975), p. 260.

2. White House Conference on Aging, *Health Care Strategies* (Washington, D.C.: U. S. Government Printing Office, Superintendent of Documents, December 1971; reprint ed., Final Report, 1973).

3. National Council on Senior Citizens, *A Platform for the Seventies for All Older Americans* (Washington, D.C.: Georgetown University Health Policy Center, May 21, 1976).

4. Tom Joe and Judy Meltzer, *Strategies for Long-Term Care* (Washington, D.C.: Georgetown University Health Policy Center, May 21, 1976).

5. Ibid.

6. Kurt Reichert, "Social Work Contributions to the Prevention of Premature Functional Death," *Human Factors in Long-Term Care* (Columbus, Oh.: National Conference on Social Welfare, Final Report of the Task Force, June 1975), pp. 9–31.

7. Jacob S. Siegel and William E. O'Leary, "Some Demographic Aspects of Aging in the United States," *Current Population Reports* (Department of Commerce, Social and Economic Statistics Administration, Bureau of the Census, Series P-23, No. 43, 1973), p. 1.

8. Louis Harris and Associates, *The Myth and Reality of Aging in America* (Washington, D.C.: National Council on the Aging, July 1976).

9. *Cost-Effectiveness Evaluation of the Levindale Geriatric Adult Treatment Center* (Baltimore, Md.: Levindale Geriatric Research Center, 1975), p. 43.

10. *The Community Care Organization: A Demonstration Project to Provide Alternative Care for Elderly and Disabled Persons* (Madison, Wis.: Office of the Lieutenant Governor, Wisconsin Community Care Organization, 1976).

11. *Triage: Coordinated Services to the Elderly* (Hartford, Conn.: Connecticut State Department on Aging, 1976).

12. Gerald M. Eggert, "A Community Wide Patient Assessment Ser-

vice: Final Report of the Patient Assessment Committee" (Rochester, N.Y.: Long-Term Care Program, July 1, 1976).

13. M. S. Pathy, "Day Hospitals for Geriatric Patients," *The Lancet,* vol. 2, 1969, pp. 533–535; Special Committee on Aging, U. S. Senate, *Adult Day Facilities for Treatment, Health Care and Related Services* (Washington, D.C.: U. S. Government Printing Office, September 1976), pp. 82–83; William Weissert, "Adult Day Care in the U. S.: A Comparative Study," report funded by contract #HRA-B6-74-148 (Rockville, Md.: National Center for Health Services Research, Health Resources Administration, Public Health Service, Department of Health, Education and Welfare, 1975).

Useful Readings

Bell, William G., "Community Care for the Elderly: An Alternative to Institutionalization," *The Gerontologist,* vol. 13, part 1, pp. 349–354.

Levey, Samuel, and Stotsky, Bernard, "Issues in Planning for Geriatric Services," *Journal of the American Geriatric Society,* vol. 17, no. 15, May 1969, pp. 459–468.

Special Committee on Aging, U. S. Senate, *Publication List* (Washington, D.C.: U. S. Government Printing Office, January 1976).

2

Day Care Programs
in Other Countries

Introduction

In order to better understand the potential for geriatric day care services in the United States, it is helpful to review their progress in other countries where they have been developing for many years. Social ideologies on which such services are based differ among countries; this accounts for the various methods and approaches to long-term care and, hence, the development of geriatric day care.

This chapter discusses the background for the day care movement in northern Europe generally, and in certain European countries in detail. Developments in other countries are also treated.

Europe

There has been a rapid development of geriatric health care in Europe. As in the United States, interest has been prompted by lack of security for the elderly due to urbanization, the breakdown of the extended family, and economic instability.

Further stimulus for the development of geriatric services comes from the high percentage of European older people with disabilities. Surveys in several countries have demonstrated that the elderly think nothing can be done about their problems and do not request help; therefore, their disabilities tend to be underreported.[1]

The course of development of services for the elderly is surprisingly similar in all parts of Europe. Society first starts institutions for the poor elderly (work houses). Soon a visiting physician is allotted; next comes nursing care institutions. Then, as this becomes too expensive, both because medical services achieve postponement of death and because these institutions provide great benefits, not only for the patient but also for his family, we start to develop day hospitals and day centers and gradually we try to revert to and develop domiciliary care and services and directly to improve the situation in the local community, where we started and probably should always remain.[2]

European geriatric services, being long-term, differ from the acute-care approach of the United States. A work group on geriatric care of the World Health Organization underlines the need for integrated social/medical approaches such as in the European System:

To be beneficial and effective, assistance must always be based on an analysis of the reasons for the existence of the need or demand for services. Otherwise it is possible that our good intentions will be harmful rather than helpful to the situation, particularly if we try to solve non-medical problems by medical methods and techniques. The importance of medical factors can easily be overemphasized because individuals often mention medical problems first, this being easier and more acceptable. There may, however, be underlying social and economic problems of greater importance.[3]

The emphasis is on reaching a homeostasis among the patient, the community, and the family. The attempt is to have decisions and responsibility for care decentralized as far as possible. Therefore, the long-term care options available to the elderly in such countries as Great Britain, Denmark, and Sweden include services provided in the homes of individual patients; innovative, noninstitutional living arrangements; and day services that patients receive in a central location.

Geriatric day care is properly viewed as only one option in a wide spectrum of services. Several modalities of day care center have developed in Europe. Depending on their source of development, each emphasizes one of the following areas: social work, medical (physician and/or nurse), psychiatric, occupational therapy, physical therapy. Table 2.1 shows this relationship.

Great Britain, Denmark, and Sweden typify developments in

Table 2.1   European Geriatric Day Centers

Modality	Emphasis	Source
Social/health center	Social work	Welfare services/ social day centers
Day hospital	Physical therapy	Medical services/ rehabilitation centers
Day hospital	Occupational therapy	Medical services/ general hospitals
Day hospital	Medical	Medical services/ nursing homes
Psychosocial center	Occupational therapy	Psychiatric hospitals

countries.[4] The following discussions are based in part on observations made during a World Health Organization Fellowship in 1974.[5]

Great Britain

Day hospitals are widely accepted and have a long history in Great Britain. There is a variety of geriatric day care models, including day clubs (social interaction centers for independent, healthy older people), day hospitals, and medical treatment and rehabilitation centers for those with physical or emotional disabilities. The British experience in day care can be most useful in the development of similar services in the United States.

It is generally agreed that the pioneering effort in day treatment was in the area of psychiatric day hospitals. (Interestingly, the first psychiatric day hospital ever developed was in Moscow, in about 1920, as a result of an emphasis on treating as many patients as possible outside the hospital.) There is some disagreement about the date of development of the first psychiatric day hospital in Great Britain. Farndale[6] places it in 1932, while Lorenze[7] dates it in 1942. The first day hospital in London, the Marlborough Day Hospital,[8] opened in 1946.

Day hospitals designed specially for the treatment of geriatric patients as a distinct group developed somewhat later and more

13

slowly, but essentially for the same reasons. In Great Britain, geriatric day hospitals grew out of the occupational therapy departments of general hospitals. The usual pattern in early geriatric day hospitals was for a few outpatients to attend hospital wards and rehabilitation departments for day treatment and return to their homes in the late afternoons.[9] The Oxford Day Hospital, which started along these lines in 1952, is generally accepted as the first geriatric day hospital in Great Britain.[10] This same arrangement for day patients was known to be in operation during the 1950s in a number of other British hospitals, but it has not proved to be satisfactory.

In 1958, Dr. Lionel Cosin opened the first geriatric day hospital built for that purpose in Cowley Road Hospital, Oxford. This day hospital had been in operation since 1952 using the existing wards and departments of the general hospital. The major innovation in 1958 was building a separate facility for the day hospital, assigning separate staff, and treating the day patients as a group. Because of the central role the Cowley Road Day Hospital has occupied as the first separate geriatric day hospital in Great Britain, it is important to describe it in some detail.

The origin of the day hospital in the occupational therapy department was evident at the Cowley Road Day Hospital both in treatment offered and in the staffing pattern. The treatment emphasis was on activities of daily living, crafts, and group activity, although physical therapy, meals, bathing, social activities, and estimation of social competence were also available. The full-time staff of the day hospital was composed primarily of occupational therapists and orderlies, with clerical services and part-time physical therapy, speech therapy, social work, and medical supervision available from the main hospital. This day hospital was organized on the concept that once an elderly person has recovered from the acute state of illness, he or she frequently can return home with some supervision. Among the advantages of the Cowley Road Day Hospital cited by Farndale are that it enabled some patients to be discharged from the hospital earlier, it assisted patients with social problems, and it provided relief for the relatives of some elderly patients.[11]

The admission process begins with a referral, usually from the patient's general practitioner. Some patients are referred directly from the geriatric unit of the hospital. To be eligible for admission, patients must be 65 or older and must have a physical and/or mental disability that does not require 24-hour skilled care. On admission, each patient receives a comprehensive examination to evaluate his or her competence in domestic, economic, social, and physical activities.[12] The need for assessment in these four areas follows logically from the goal of enabling patients to maintain themselves in the community. The patient's competence in these four areas is reevaluated monthly by an interdisciplinary treatment team. Most patients continue to attend this particular day hospital for more than 12 months. Estimated cost for five-day attendance in 1974 was 15 pounds per patient (approximately $45 per week).

Just before the opening of the Cowley Road Day Hospital, a British government report defined the objectives of day hospitals as follows: to prevent or retard physical or mental deterioration of patients, to assist in the therapeutic management of patients, to help relieve the strain on patients' relatives, and to avoid excessive occupation of hospital beds.[13] In his 1958–59 survey of British day hospitals, Farndale identified 10 geriatric day hospitals. At this time, geriatric day hospitals were considered experimental services and were usually small and limited in scope. The geriatric day hospital movement grew rapidly between 1959 and 1970, by which time there were at least 120 geriatric day hospitals in the United Kingdom.[14] This rapid expansion occurred because the early programs demonstrated the need for day service in geriatric care. The generally accepted advantages of day hospital services include:

1. more efficient use of inpatient beds because of earlier discharge of some patients and prevention of inpatient admission of others;

2. retention of patients in the community during medical treatment, thus reducing the danger of institutionalization for these patients and utilizing existing family and community ties in the therapeutic process;

3. relief provided to the families of elderly patients;

4. increased social contact for socially isolated patients;

5. economy of care compared to institutional care.[15]

In 1971, the Department of Health and Social Security provided guidelines for the operation of day hospital programs. According to this document, "The planning and operation of day hospitals may now be said to have passed through the experimental stage and the time may now be appropriate for detailed advice on the planning and operation of day hospitals based on the effective and efficient practices developed in recent years."[16] The official recommendation was that day hospitals be considered an integral part of the geriatric services because of their significant contribution to the total care of the elderly, as well as their improvement of the effectiveness of inpatient care.[17]

An appropriate population for day hospitals was defined as patients for whom it is hoped to delay or avoid admission to hospitals as inpatients, patients who need careful follow-up after discharge from a hospital, patients awaiting hospital admission who can begin investigation and treatment, and inpatients nearing discharge from a hospital for whom the transition from inpatient to community living can be smoothed.[18] It is interesting to note that the last two reasons for admission are unique to Great Britain and are not emphasized in the United States or other countries.

Two day-hospital places per 1,000 elderly population (65 years and older) was the average provision suggested by the Department of Health and Social Security.[19] This rate was reported to vary, however, depending on local circumstances. A range of 20 to 40 places was the recommended size for day hospitals; larger programs were considered to be unwieldy and difficult to administer, and smaller programs tended not to be economical.

Although no ideal staff to patient ratio was identified in these guidelines, several staffing recommendations were made: The day hospital should be supervised by a consultant geriatrician, who is available to see day patients at least one day per week. One individual, usually a nurse, should be responsible for the day-to-day operation of the day hospital. Nursing staff is considered a necessity; however, much of the unskilled nursing and rehabilitation work could be done by aides under professional supervision. The importance of interdisciplinary teamwork in planning for and administering care was stressed.

Day hospital services are now considered an integral and necessary part of the long-term health care system in Great Britain. The British system does, however, distinguish between day hospitals and day centers. The Cowley Road facility, described above, exemplifies the day hospital, while Parkfield Hall in Stockton, in the County Borough of Teeside, exemplifies the day center. Parkfield Hall Day Centre is located in a new house built for that purpose. The center is open five days a week. Thirty places a day are available and most members attend two days a week. Salaried staff include an organizer-director, secretary, and two drivers.

Voluntary assistance is utilized very heavily at this day center. Volunteers are recruited from women's clubs, church groups, and schools. The absence of medical staff accentuates the social nature of the services of this day center. Services include assistance with personal care such as bathing and hairdressing; social activities; lunch and tea; and regular excursions.

There are no government guidelines for the operation of day centers.

Day Hospital versus Day Center

The distinction made between the day hospital and day center is relevant to current debate in the United States about the medical versus social role. In Great Britain, these services operate on the same general principle: to provide care to elderly persons with physical, mental, or social impairments on a day basis, with the patients maintaining their homes in the community and returning there in the evening.[20] The major differences are in the auspices, staffing patterns, scope and variety of services, characteristics of patients served, and expected outcomes of treatment. Although a rather clear distinction has been made between the day hospital and the day center, in practice the differences between these units tend to blur and the services tend to overlap.[21] Table 2.2 summarizes the differences between the British day hospital and day center.

The day hospital is operated under the auspices of the Hospital Authority (responsible for medical services). In general, day hospitals are closely associated with geriatric or general hospitals and have access to the medical facilities of these hospitals.[22] The overall emphasis of the day hospital is on medical diagnosis, treatment, and rehabilitation. Thus, the day hospital is equipped for diagnosis or assessment of those patients who do not need to be admitted on an inpatient basis but cannot be adequately assessed as outpatients, as well as for medical and nursing treatment for any condition that does

Table 2.2 Conceptual Distinctions between the
British Day Hospital and Day Center

Variables	Day Hospital	Day Center
Auspices	Hospital authority closely associated with geriatric or general hospital	Local authority or voluntary organization
Staffing	Salaried professional staff and aides	Salaried or volunteer staff or combination—no professionals required
Service emphasis	Medical	Social
Services	Diagnosis and evaluation; medical and nursing treatment; rehabilitation treatment (physical therapy, occupational therapy, speech therapy)	Social interaction, minimal supervision and custodial care, meals, bathing, occupational therapy at some centers
Patient characteristics	More seriously disabled patients who do not need 24-hour skilled care and can benefit from active treatment	Less-seriously disabled patients in need of social stimulation and minimal supervision
Expected patient outcome	Rehabilitation to higher level of functioning	Maintenance at current level of functioning; prevention of deterioration
Location	Usually in long-term care hospitals	Old people's homes or free standing
Days of operation	Five to seven days a week	Five to seven days a week
Cost to patient	Usually none	Cost varies with locality

not require skilled care around the clock.[23] Social interaction opportunities generally are considered not as a primary purpose of day hospital care but as a beneficial side-effect. The patient population of the day hospital is defined by the available services and functions.

Patients are expected to benefit from medical treatment by resident physicians and to be amenable to rehabilitation or at least maintenance of functioning through active treatment. Thus, the day hospital is neither a custodian nor a holding center for patients.

Day centers, on the other hand, are operated under the auspices of local authorities (responsible for social welfare services) or voluntary organizations. The ratios of paid staff and volunteers to patients vary. The emphasis of the day center is on the provision of social stimulation of participants and it serves as a holding center with supervisory and custodial functions. Most day centers provide company, meals, bath, chiropody, and occupational therapy. Participants receive necessary medical care from their own physicians.

Center participants are supposed to be less likely to benefit from short-term rehabilitation and treatment. Attendance at the day center may continue for many months. Farndale[24] characterizes day center participants as "frail elderly" persons who are not able to maintain complete independence in the community or whose families need assistance in caring for them.

It can be seen from the definitions above that day hospitals and day centers are separate parts of a continuum of health care for geriatric patients. Several authors have suggested that an ideal relationship between the two forms of day care would be one in which a central day hospital could be served by several day centers.[25] When day hospital patients improved to the point that they no longer needed medical treatment, they could be discharged to one of the day centers. There, they could receive the social stimulation and supervision necessary to maintain the level of functioning achieved in the day hospital. One reason for current retention of inappropriate patients in day hospitals is the lack of such coordinated services.

Although social day centers are available in only 55 percent of the areas surveyed by Brocklehurst, it is interesting to note that they were three times more common in areas served by a day hospital. In the areas where both existed, they seem to have developed together.[26] Since discharge from a day hospital is made easier by the presence of a day center, it may be that the day hospitals created, or made more obvious, a demand for social day care. The observation is supported by the authors' experience in the United States.

Denmark

The county governments and the Corporation of Copenhagen are responsible for the administration of health services in Denmark. Long-term care became part of the Danish health care system in the 1960s under national health insurance benefits. At that time, Denmark began to develop day care center facilities along the British model; these were called day nursing homes.

The day nursing home is a relatively new development in the long-term care system of Denmark. These homes provide a higher level of care than social day centers, and are open seven days a week. Day nursing homes are now being required by law in Denmark and are similar to day hospitals in Great Britain. The cost for day care services in 1974 was 300 Kr (approximately $50.70) per patient day, compared to 400 Kr per patient in a nursing home and 700 to 1,400 Kr per patient in a hospital. Patients were charged 10.5 Kr (approximately $1.80) per day for day nursing homes.

The Peder Lykke Center, in Copenhagen, is a multipurpose geriatric center.[27] It is described in some detail here because it is an innovative delivery system that offers a number of service options in one complex of buildings. This system allows individuals to move from one level of care to another with minimal disturbance. The Peder Lykke Center is operated jointly by the Lonely Old People's Aid *(Ensomme Gamles Vaern)*, a private organization, and the Corporation of Copenhagen, the city government. There are three principal components of the Peder Lykke Center: service flats, nursing flats, and day nursing homes. Old people from the surrounding community, the service flats, and the nursing flats participate in the activities of the day center.

The primary aim of the day center is to improve and maintain the physical and mental health of participants through intellectual, manual, and club activities, such as courses in cultural and practical topics, occupational therapy (participants may sell their craft items at a central shop), and social gatherings and entertainments. Day center staff are available for counseling on social, personal, and health problems. The center also offers a home visiting service and facilities for bathing, chiropody, and hairdressing. The inclusion of well and active individuals from the surrounding community is considered an important factor in the operation of the day center. This introduction to the Peder Lykke Center may ease the transition of community residents to the service or nursing flats, if this is necessary. It also puts residents of the nursing flats in closer touch with the community than might otherwise be possible.

Although Denmark's day care centers are only a decade old, they are well established in the country. The fact that only 2.5 percent of old-age pensioners in Denmark are in nursing homes compared to about five percent in the United States attests to the success of Denmark's day care and geriatric programs. It is estimated that 50 percent of the patients attending day care centers would be inpatients if not for the centers.[28]

Sweden

Striking evidence of the need for geriatric care was disclosed in a 1950 survey by the Swedish government showing that the elderly were being warehoused in poor houses and nursing homes.[29] The government decided that something had to be done; not only was it a national disgrace, but resources were being poured into this "poor relief system" and too few benefits were being obtained from it. The elderly were occupying three times as many hospital beds as the rest of the population, even though they made up only 20 percent of the population. In 1951, the Swedish County Councils were given responsibility for the care of the chronically ill, putting this care on an equal footing with medical care.

Medical care in Sweden is financed primarily through county income taxes; the individual patient pays only a small portion of the cost of care at the time of illness. All Swedish citizens, as well as others who live and work in Sweden, are covered by the National Insurance Act, which provides compensation for income lost because of illness as well as for medical care and related expenses.[30]

It is only in the last few years that priority has been given to the place of long-term care in the Swedish health care system.[31] Until recently, emphasis had been on the provision of health care on an inpatient basis. One reason for this is that specialist care was provided mostly by hospitals so that many patients had to be admitted because of the distance of specialist care from their homes. Long-term care began as a separate specialty in 1969. There has also been a concomitant emphasis on preventive medicine services, which now account for about 10 percent of the health budget.[32]

In view of the relatively short history of long-term care and the emphasis on inpatient care, it is not surprising that day care in Sweden is also new and not as widely available as in Great Britain or Denmark. The most common day care setting is the day ward, which is actually quite similar to the British day hospital. Services emphasize physical therapy (especially hydrotherapy—several wards have elaborate facilities including swimming pools), instead of occupational therapy. The charge to the patient for day ward services in 1974 was 12 Kr (approximately $2.10) per day, the same charge as for an outpatient visit. No cost data were available on day ward services.

In 1969, one of the first Swedish geriatric day wards, the Langbro Day Center, opened near Stockholm. This center is a psychogeriatric center affiliated with a psychiatric hospital. It has two units with six staff members assigned to each. The primary objective stated by the staff of the program is to prevent institutionalization and regression.

In 1974 there were 38 "guests" enrolled in the Langbro Center, with an average daily attendance of 20 to 25. The center is open Monday through Friday, and each guest may attend from one to five days per week. Frequency of attendance is decided by the director and the guests. There is no waiting list for this center because the staff refers all persons who cannot be accommodated.

The admission process usually begins with a patient referral through the social service department. Most patients come to the center from the community; only a few are referred directly from inpatient wards. All staff participate in each initial assessment and intake process. Most patients continue to participate in the center for several months.

Services include psychological testing, occupational therapy, and group interaction opportunities. Group contact is considered one of the most important therapeutic services. The program is relatively unstructured; various activities are available, but there is no rigid schedule. Patients arrive at the center at approximately 9 A.M., are served breakfast and lunch, and leave for home at about 3 P.M.

The geriatric day care program at the Uppsala Hospital is another day ward that opened in 1969. By 1974, when 60 patients were enrolled, with 20 patients attending each day, staff indicated that three times the available places were needed, as well as additional staff and space. The average stay for day patients in this program is six months to one year. The staff consists of a nurse, a subnurse, and two helpers. This represents a staff to patient ratio of one to five, which is average among such day wards.

Three levels of care are available on Uppsala's day ward: individual physical therapy and occupational therapy, self-training and group training, and monthly open house visits for discharged patients. This last level is a rather interesting concept; the day ward maintains some contact with discharged patients to facilitate readmission and to continue support and social interaction. Similar day wards operate at Valla Hospital in Linköping and at Vårbergs Hospital in Skörholmen.[33]

In summary, the Swedish day care services, although not very developed, are accepted as part of the health care system and are based on an open care approach that emphasizes matching services to the patient's needs.[34]

Other Countries

Robins[35] concludes in a report on day hospitals in Israel that although they are regarded as a vital aspect of care, such programs are still in the formative stages. The problems cited in program development are transportation and data collection to document costs, utilization, and diagnostic categories. Four day care programs (similar to the British day hospital) were operating in Israel in 1975.

Letters of inquiry were sent by the authors to 15 countries (Australia, Bangladesh, Hong Kong, India, Indonesia, Japan, Korea, Malaysia, Nepal, New Guinea, Philippines, Republic of China, Republic of Viet Nam, Singapore, and Thailand). Responses failed to provide any information indicating that services similar to geriatric day care centers existed in any of these countries.

23

Notes

1. A. N. Exton-Smith, "Geriatrics and the National Health Service," a paper on the Social and Clinical Aspects of Geriatric Medicine and the National Picture (London: St. Pancras Hospital, 1968); Gudmund Harlem, "The Health Protection of the Elderly," a paper presented at the World Health Organization, Regional Committee for Europe, Technical Discussions 24, Bucharest, Rumania, September 10–14, 1974.

2. Gudmund Harlem, "The Health Protection of the Elderly," a paper presented at the World Health Organization, Regional Committee for Europe, Technical Discussions 24, Bucharest, Rumania, September 10–14, 1974.

3. *Summary Report,* Working Group on Rehabilitation in Long-Term and Geriatric Care, World Health Organization, Copenhagen, Denmark, February 18–22, 1974.

4. E. G. Robins, "Day Care in Sweden, Denmark and Holland: Applicability to Programs in the U.S.," a paper presented at the Gerontological Society meeting, New York, N.Y., October 14, 1976.

5. P. G. Weiler, "Geriatric Delivery Systems: European and American Models," Final Report of World Health Organization Fellowship, February 1975.

6. James Farndale, *The Day Hospital Movement in Great Britain* (New York: Pergamon Press, 1961).

7. Edward J. Lorenze, "The Day Hospital: An Alternative to Institutional Care," *Journal of the American Geriatric Society,* vol. 22, no. 7, July 1974, pp. 316–320.

8. James Farndale, *The Day Hospital Movement in Great Britain* (New York: Pergamon Press: 1961).

9. J. C. Brocklehurst, *The Geriatric Day Hospital* (London: King Edwards Hospital Fund, 1970).

10. J. Andrews, "A Geriatric Day Ward in an English Hospital," *Journal of the American Geriatric Society,* vol. 18, no. 5, May 1970, pp. 378–386.

11. James Farndale, *The Day Hospital Movement in Great Britain* (New York: Pergamon Press, 1961).

12. L. Z. Cosin, "Rehabilitation of the Older Patient," *World Hospitals,* vol. 9, edition 4, October 1973.

13. M. E. J. Wadsworth, "A Geriatric Day Hospital and Its Systems of Care," *Social Science and Medicine*, vol. 6, 1972, pp. 507–525.

14. James Farndale, *The Day Hospital Movement in Great Britain* (New York: Pergamon Press, 1961).

15. J. C. Brocklehurst, "Role of Day Hospital Care," *British Medical Journal*, vol. 4, 1973, pp. 223–225.

16. "Geriatric Day Hospitals" (London: Department of Health and Social Security, reference F/G 54/17, December 7, 1971).

17. Ibid.

18. Ibid.

19. Ibid., p. 8.

20. D. B. Rao, "Day Hospitals and Welfare Homes in the Care of the Aged," *Journal of the American Geriatric Society*, vol. 19, no. 9, 1971, pp. 781–787.

21. M. S. Pathy, "Day Hospitals for Geriatric Patients," *The Lancet*, vol. 2, 1969, pp. 533–535; Woodford-Williams, "The Day Hospital in the Community Care of the Elderly," *Gerontologia Clinica*, vol. 4, 1962, pp. 241–256.

22. E. V. B. Morton, "Advance in Geriatrics," *The Practitioner*, vol. 203, 1969, pp. 525–534.

23. J. R. Wilkie, "Day Hospitals and Day Centres in an English County," *Proceedings of the Royal Society of Medicine*, vol. 67, 1974, pp. 677–680.

24. James Farndale, *The Day Hospital Movement in Great Britain* (New York: Pergamon Press, 1961).

25. J. C. Brocklehurst, "Role of Day Hospital Care," *British Medical Journal*, vol. 4, 1973, pp. 223–225; L. Z. Cosin, "The Place of the Day Hospital in the Geriatric Unit," *The Practitioner*, vol. 172, 1954, pp. 552–559; J. R. Wilkie, "Day Hospitals and Day Centres in an English County," *Proceedings of the Royal Society of Medicine*, vol. 67, 1974, pp. 667–680.

26. J. C. Brocklehurst, *The Geriatric Day Hospital* (London: King Edwards Hospital Fund, 1970).

27. The Peder Lykke Centre, EGV, *Lonely Old People's Aid*. A booklet prepared by the Corporation of Copenhagen and Ensomme Gamles Vaern, Denmark, January 1974.

28. Bent Furstnow-Sorensen, *Care of the Old: Social Conditions in Denmark 2* (Copenhagen, Denmark: Ministries of Labor and Social Affairs, International Relations Division, 1970).

29. Hans Zetterqvist, "Social Welfare for the Elderly in Sweden," a lecture given at the World Health Organization course on the Medical and Social Aspects of the Care of the Elderly, Kiev, USSR, June 1968.

30. *Fact Sheets on Sweden: The Organization of Medical Care in Sweden* (Stockholm, Sweden: The Swedish Institute, FS76 D Vpb, November 1973); S. A. Lindgren, "Sweden," in *Health Service Prospects: An International Survey* (London: The Lancet and the Nuffield Provincial Hospitals Trust, 1973).

31. Lars Linder, *Factors to Consider in Long Term Care*, unpublished paper (Uppsala, Sweden: Kungsgardets Hospital, September 1974).

32. Budd Shenkin, "Politics and Medical Care in Sweden: The Seven Crowns Reform," *The New England Journal of Medicine*, vol. 228, no. 11, 1973, pp. 555–559.

33. P. G. Weiler, "Geriatric Delivery Systems: European and American Models," Final Report of World Health Organization Fellowship, February 1975.

34. Hans Zetterqvist, "The Social Welfare for the Elderly in Sweden," a lecture given at the World Health Organization course on the Medical and Social Aspects of the Care of the Elderly, Kiev, USSR, June 1968.

35. Edith G. Robins, "Report on Day Hospitals in Israel and Great Britain" (Rockville, Maryland: Health Resources Administration, Division of Long-Term Care, Department of Health, Education and Welfare, October 15, 1975).

Useful Readings

Silver, C. P., "A Jointly Sponsored Geriatric Social Club and Day Hospital," *Gerontologia Clinica*, vol. 12, 1970, pp. 235–240.

Woodford-Williams, E., and Alvarez, A. S., "Four Years of Experience of a Day Hospital in Geriatric Practice," *Gerontologia Clinica*, vol. 7, 1965, pp. 96–106.

3

Day Care Programs
in the United States

Introduction

There are about 170 adult day care centers in the United States, many of which are newly opened.[1] This slow growth can be attributed mainly to the unanticipated and now unwanted consequences of private health insurance and public policies (Medicare and Medicaid, enacted in 1965) that favored paying only for institutional care to discourage frivolous entry into the health care system. For many years, many services commonly needed by aged adults (diagnosis, supervision, assistance with activities of daily living) could be reimbursed only if obtained in an institutional setting such as a hospital or nursing home. Home care services usually were not reimbursed unless they followed release from an inpatient facility.

But as health care costs, particularly institutional costs, began to threaten the public purse, alternatives were sought. Late in 1972, Congress formally directed the Secretary of the Department of Health, Education, and Welfare (DHEW) to undertake a search for alternatives. The law (P.L. 92–603) specified that adult day care would be one of the alternatives considered.

Several efforts were mounted by DHEW to carry out the congressional mandate; among them was the funding of a study by the Transcentury Corporation of 10 existing adult day care programs. This was a first attempt at describing what this new care mode, American style, consisted of.[2] The latter portion of this chapter summarizes its findings.

The Growth of Day Care Services in the United States

The United States has been characterized by one of its best-known sociologists, Amitai Etzioni, as a country whose entire social history has been spent in "turning over ever more functions once discharged by the family to corporate bodies or institutions."[3] But even Etzioni admits that there is more to the last decade's growth of various long-term care institutions than simply a flaw in our social fabric. Like others, he refers to public support of these facilities as a factor in their growth.

Etzioni describes reimbursement rules as operating on an "open-ticket basis: the more people in, the more funds shelled out."[4] DHEW's Social Security Administration is not ready to admit to all the blame or to acknowledge any "open ticket" qualities of public payments, but spokesmen do agree that Medicare and Medicaid have had an important influence: "Following the enactment of Medicare and Medicaid, many large new facilities were built and many older, smaller ones were forced to close or modernize and expand to meet the upgraded standards of the new program."[5] This is at best an understatement. By just half a dozen years after passage of Medicare, the number of nursing home beds in service had tripled to about 944,700 beds in some 13,200 facilities.[6] Latest figures (from 1974) show the trend continuing at a still considerable, if somewhat more reasonable, rate.[7]

Much of this growth and upgrading may have been expected and even desired. Indeed, in his authoritative history of Medicare's early years, Witkin asserts that the whole purpose of Medicare was to cover inpatient services, not ambulatory care. Coverage of these additional benefits (under what is now known as Part B of the act) was "just thrown in" during the congressional fight over the bill, he reports. The intent and effect was to "upgrade" existing facilities and encourage construction of new ones:

> To many of our senior citizens, the nursing home was a place they went to die. It was an ambivalent situation. The home offered custodial care at various levels, but it offered little hope to the individual in the form of medical treatment for a better tomorrow. The widening of institutional concepts to include the "subacute hospital" was a very significant one to the patient himself. It also served to upgrade the level of care available even in the nursing home.[8]

Such impact upon quality of care and facilities has always been a major contribution of public assistance to previously privately supported care industries. Reichert traces this trend back to the period just after World War II, when both physicians and housing were in sufficiently short supply to spur the growth of a cottage industry of nursing care in the nation's large cities.

A wife caring for her husband might find that she could just as easily take care of a few more old sick people. A next step to a larger institution became the logical choice of those who were more aggressive albeit not necessarily those with entrepreneurial or management skills. Often used as a placement of last resort, facilities had little control over the levels of care. Newspaper scandals about quality of care led to controls by some states, carried out mainly, however, in terms of fire prevention and building safety. Welfare departments increased their financial involvement as they paid for client care directly and later through the federal Medical Assistance program. Not long after the Hill-Burton program started in 1946, government began guarantees for private loans which made it easier for the nonprofit and later the proprietary home, even in the poorer states, to build more beds. Gradually, nursing home operators came to feel assured of ongoing financial support.

In 1965, Medicare arrived and its extended care facility reimbursement encouraged upgrading of skilled nursing.[9]

By early in this decade, we had come full circle. Changing standards of quality (of life as well as care) made nursing home care even under the best circumstances a less desirable alternative than continued participation as an active family member and community member living in a private home:

Deinstitutionalization has affected decidedly the current scene. This has resulted from and has been influenced by, among other developments, the growth of community mental health centers and of community educational efforts for the retarded; research on the negative impact of institutional life on all personalities regardless of illness, problem, or handicap; and state decisions to be relieved of expensive long-term care for the mentally ill and the mentally retarded through transfer to federally supported local programs.[10]

Part of the problem was the abhorrent care standards of some nursing homes, described by the U.S. Senate Subcommittee on Long-Term Care as "the litany of nursing home abuses."[11] Patients were

29

ignored by physicians, beaten, drugged, robbed, and neglected, the committee reported.

Yet the costs continued to go up: Federal outlays under Medicare rose by 78 percent between 1968 and 1973—from $5.3 billion to $9.5 billion.[12] To combat these cost, quality, and other problems and to respond to growing criticism of unnecessary and excessive institutionalization, several initiatives were undertaken by the executive branch.[13] In 1971, President Nixon began the efforts with a message to Congress calling for a series of changes known as the Nursing Home Improvement Program. Congress responded with amendments to the relevant sections of the Medicare and Medicaid laws to allow DHEW to create unified standards and regulations governing skilled nursing facilities.

An Office of Nursing Home Affairs was established within DHEW and, in January, 1974, uniform federal regulations were published governing participation by skilled nursing facilities and intermediate care facilities in the Medicare and Medicaid programs. Finally, beginning in 1974 in response to a congressional mandate specified in the 1972 amendments to the Medicare law, a series of experiments and demonstrations was undertaken to test the viability of new approaches to rendering and paying for care. Several of these approaches focused on finding ambulatory alternatives to institutional care. Among these, adult day care was prominently listed.[14]

The Growth of Community-Based Alternatives

Debate has only begun over what may constitute true "alternatives" to institutional care. Trager makes the point that, when the need for institutional care is a valid one, there is no such thing as an alternative.[15] Hence, what are now being called alternatives are in reality a new range of services. The range is quite broad.

The most common combination for the largest group of consumers is: regular supervision; part-time paraprofessionals who provide the essential supports and therapeutic regimes when activities of daily living and the capacity for self-care are temporarily or permanently limited; social services for assessment, ongoing individual care, and utilization of community resources; physical, speech, and occupational therapy; nutritional counseling; recreation; and transportation, when needed. To these basics, expanded programs have added telephone reassurance, meals-on-wheels, friendly visiting, and the use of day hospitals and adult day care centers.

Though multipurpose clubs or congeries have been in existence since man became communal, those who have done research on the growth in the United States of such groupings exclusively for the elderly date them only as far back as 1870 in Boston.[16] The first actual multiservice *center* exclusively for the elderly is even more recent. It opened in New York City less than 30 years ago.[17] But such centers grew rapidly, so that by 1962 there were more than 500. Their nature has varied so widely that it remains a difficult task to characterize all of them briefly. Maxwell found it easiest to separate them into two basic groups: single service and multiservice.

There are three types of single service centers:

Recreation or education centers: These centers are set up under the aegis of a public department of recreation or education. The staff is trained for recreation, or for education as the case may be. It is not their function to be concerned about health, housing, economic, or other needs of people, nor are they equipped by training or experience to handle these other needed services or referrals.

Drop-in centers: Some centers are maintained as a place to which older people may come to sit, to talk, to meet others casually. These are seen as "community living rooms." The staff, if any, performs custodial duties. Little or no program is carried on.

Information and referral centers: These centers usually are located in a central downtown office. They provide information about available services for older people.[18]

Multiservice centers contrast sharply with all these and, to make the distinction, they are often called adult day care centers. The unique feature of this type of center is a concern for the older person as a whole person, in all aspects of his or her life. The staff needs to be greater in proportion to membership, and may include people from a variety of professional disciplines, such as social group workers and case workers, adult educators, recreation workers, doctors, nurses, employment counselors, dietitians, craftsmen, and musicians.

Most of the multiservice centers stress the maintenance or enhancement of physical, social, and emotional well-being. Centers whose emphases are restorative or rehabilitative are most frequently related to a hospital, a home for the aged, or a health department.[19]

Transcentury Study

Successors to the Maxwell study have concentrated on those facilities known as senior centers, which Maxwell described as tending less frequently to offer health care, and therefore to staff accordingly. A national study, conducted by the Transcentury Corporation and sponsored by the National Center for Health Services Research under P.L. 92–603,[20] considered adult day care as a possible benefit of Medicare coverage. It dealt exclusively with health-oriented programs, all of which were known either as adult day care centers or as day hospitals. A detailed discussion of this study provides a comprehensive overview of day care in the United States. The study got underway in mid-1974, using as a sample 10 programs in eight states representing as broad a mix as possible of urban and rural settings, organizational affiliations, program sizes, lengths of operation, and ethnicity of participants. The report described and compared the principal characteristics of these 10 prototypical programs, showing a wide variety of adult day programs in terms of patients served, differences in program objectives and services, alternative staffing patterns, and costs per patient-day.

Data Collection

Data came from site visits to all programs. A typical visit lasted roughly three days (except at programs with multiple sites, where visits lasted roughly four days), and required the services of a three- to five-member team that spent roughly nine person-days (12 person-days at multisite programs) reducing and reporting the data for subsequent comparative analysis. Brief revisits were necessary in some cases. Data collection visits were organized around five protocols either developed expressly for this study or adapted for this study from an existing instrument. Table 3.1 lists the programs with some of the characteristics they contributed to the selected sample.

Comparison of the 10 Centers

Judging from the 10 centers, adult day care is often initiated in one of two ways: Either some gap in existing services to the impaired elderly is recognized and an adult day care center is developed specifically to fill it, or, less frequently, someone in the community in a position to influence health care program decisions learns about the concept of adult day care and promotes a center. Centers developed to fill a specific service gap had a clear sense of mission and an idea of where the service fit in the long-term care continuum.

Burke, St. Camillus, and St. Otto's are examples of adult day care programs initiated in response to a need for service. The planning staff of the Burke Rehabilitation Center had discovered that some of its patients who were sufficiently recuperated to justify release from inpatient status but still in need of ambulatory rehabilitative care couldn't get such care locally. Burke Day Hospital now fills the gap, strongly favoring for admission those who need rehabilitative care. Its participants are primarily fracture and stroke victims. At St. Camillus, the outpatient department administrator had found that outpatients still needed, but could not get, some of the support services they had received as inpatients. St. Otto's was pulled into a gap in the Minnesota mental health care system as the volume of discharges from the state's mental institutions rose and the dearth of suitable ambulatory care facilities for the mentally ill became more profound.

San Diego and Montefiore are examples of the other type of program origin: where the idea preceded the program. In San Diego, a member of the county's board of supervisors was asked during a television interview what services were being sponsored for the aged in the county. The supervisor cited adult day care as an example. A community service agency for the elderly was then called upon to draft an idea paper on adult day care. What emerged was a broad program offering a wide range of services to a variety of elderly individuals. Emphasis is on social support services, but medical, health, and therapy services are available on referral or from a team of specialists. Most participants need rehabilitative or maintenance care. The Montefiore program was designed after officials were told

Table 3.1 Adult Day Care Centers Selected for Transcentury Study

Center	Average Daily Attendance*	Principal Funding Source	Months in Operation	Affiliation	Days per Week in Operation	Location
Tucson Senior Health Improvement Programs	115	Model Cities	92	Nursing home/hospital	5	Tucson, Ariz.
San Diego Senior Adult Day Care Program	52	Revenue Sharing	20	Social service organization	5	San Diego, Calif.
On Lok Senior Health Services Center	47	Title IV, OAA	27	Free standing	7	San Francisco, Calif.
Burke Day Hospital	40	Title IV, OAA	27	Rehabilitation Center	5	White Plains, N. Y.
Lexington Center for Creative Living	29	Title VI, SSA	25	County health department	5	Lexington, Ky.
Mosholu-Montefiore Geriatric Day Care Program	28	Title IV, OAA	26	YMHA-YWHA/hospital	5	Bronx, N. Y.
Levindale Adult Day Treatment Program	25	Medicaid	60	Geriatric center	5	Baltimore, Md.
St. Camillus Health Care by the Day Program	18	Medicaid	34	Skilled nursing facility	5	Syracuse, N. Y.
Athens-Brightwood Day Care Center	11	Title VI, SSA	36	Social service organization	5	Athens, Ga.
St. Otto's Day Care Program	11	Medicaid	79	Nursing home	5	Little Falls, Minn.

* Figures reflect study team findings of actual attendance on site visit days and program records of lunches consumed in sample months. Tucson program officials disagree with figures for their program. Their estimate is 143.

of the possibility that funding for adult day care might be available from DHEW. This left the designers free to produce a program aimed at meeting a wide variety of participant needs. Social dysfunction is sufficient for admission.

Another program, On Lok, defies categorization. Though it was designed in response to a study of deficiencies in the local long-term care delivery system, it is unique in that it was designed to fill not a specific gap but a general one. Services delivered by On Lok are the most comprehensive of the 10 programs, though many of them are social services, and though therapy services constitute a small percentage of staff time.

The Athens-Brightwood Day Care Center began operation in 1970. It originated when the homemaker/home health service agency thought it could provide therapeutic care at a lower cost in a supervised group setting. The center serves an average of 11 persons per day and is affiliated with a social service organization. It maintains a contractual meal service arrangement with a local senior citizen center and has an informal affiliation with a hospital-based home health care program.

The Tucson Senior Health Improvement Programs began in 1968 as a single-site day care center whose primary objective was to prevent improper institutionalization. The program has undergone major expansion and diversification during this time and now offers services to an average of 115 persons per day. The program is part of a network of 16 day care centers in institutional and noninstitutional settings, and is coordinated by a central administration.

The Lexington and Levindale centers, discussed in detail in Chapter 4, were initiated in response to a specific gap in the community.

Physical Facilities

Quarters of the 10 adult day care programs range from luxury class to steerage. Burke and On Lok are two contrasting examples. At On Lok, participants crowd themselves and their wheelchairs into an L-shaped common activity room where arm pulleys hang from the ceiling and a T-bar exerciser stands incongruously next to the folding tables and chairs that at lunch time turn the room into a dining hall. For three or four hours in the morning, the same tables are used by the program's participants for arts and crafts, reading, arguing or chatting with friends, and just sitting quietly. Occasionally, a participant will roll his wheelchair under the arm pulleys and practice an exercise taught him or her by the center's part-time physical therapist. Meanwhile, a speech therapist battles the high-decibel din while working with a stroke victim to regain the use of voice muscles. Two more participants sleep, or at least lie quietly, on rollaway beds behind a curtain partially drawn across one end of the L-shaped room. A small, partitioned examining room tucked into one corner and a bathroom with extra wide doorways to accommodate wheelchairs confirm the impression that the cavernous room is a health facility. Once it was a neighborhood cocktail lounge.

Burke Day Hospital is quite different. Though its stout brick and stone building is as old as some of its participants, it is obviously a fully equipped modern facility with its own X-ray machine, laboratory, and therapy rooms. Backup facilities duplicating the day care center's own, plus some the center does not have, are in the Rehabilitation Center if participants need them. Actual use of these backup facilities is infrequent, however.

St. Camillus contrasts with both On Lok and Burke by being totally integrated into the services and facilities of its parent organization, an extended care facility, without any special quarters for the adult day care program.

Two others, Tucson and San Diego, share a characteristic unique to them: They are both multisite operations. Each consists of a headquarters center plus several satellite centers. At each program, one administrative unit is in charge of all centers and some staff are shared by the satellites.

Criteria for Admission to Day Care Program

Most common criteria—participant cannot be:
- bedridden,
- totally disoriented,
- potentially harmful or disruptive,
- an alcoholic or drug addict,
- without medical need,

• a resident of a mental institution,*
• a resident outside the program's catchment area, unless he or she provides transportation,
• younger than 55 years old (preferred).

Exceptions made by some programs:
• participants of all ages accepted,
• a personal physician is not required,
• persons who live in mental institutions, nursing homes, or personal care homes accepted,
• participant must be oriented to person, but not necessarily to place and time,
• participants can be disruptive, as long as they are not harmful to themselves or others.

Additional restrictions made by some programs—participants must:
• be over 60 years old,
• have a family member or family surrogate to provide supervision and care during nonprogram hours,
• be eligible for one of three levels of institutional care,
• be eligible for Medicaid or be able to pay own bills,
• not be frequently/habitually incontinent,
• not require constant supervision due to disorientation,
• be able to use a walker in an emergency, if he or she is wheelchair-bound,
• not be subject to cardiac arrest,
• not require a special diet.

Intake and Review Procedures

As with admission criteria, the programs' intake and review procedures vary widely. Every program has established these procedures, but the process and the professional backgrounds of personnel used to conduct them are quite dissimilar.

---

*St. Otto's is an exception and the effect has been profound. It began as a geriatric program but evolved into a psychiatric program after the state began massive releases of residents of mental institutions.

All of the programs request that the applicant's personal physician (if there is one) perform an initial medical evaluation, and all but one of the programs use a multidisciplinary team to prepare the participant's plan of care. The team consists at least of a nurse practitioner, a physical therapist, an occupational therapist, a speech therapist, a social worker, and a director of patient activities. However, only On Lok has a staff physician as a regular member of the final evaluation team.

Procedures common to most programs:
• Initial screening is done by registered nurse and/or social worker.
• Staff social worker obtains a social history.
• Participant's personal physician is asked for medical records and to perform an initial evaluation.
• Participant's personal physician must provide medical clearance for program activities.
• Functional assessments are conducted by the registered nurse, physical therapist, and occupational therapist.
• Final evaluation on program admission is done by interdisciplinary team, not including a physician.
• Plan of care is prepared by multidisciplinary team including at least a registered nurse and a social worker.
• There is an informal one-month trial period.
• Participant's progress is reviewed at least every six weeks.

Procedures employed by only a few programs:
• All referrals are screened initially by a central intake unit composed of social workers.
• Initial screening is conducted by social worker only.
• Initial screening is conducted by social worker and registered nurse in the applicant's home.
• If there is a need for verification of an applicant's medical status, a physician from the affiliated health facility is called in during the initial screening process.
• Applicants referred by one of the program's funding sources have already been screened by a social worker and determined eligible for day care services.

• The intake-orientation phase lasts for three to eight weeks, during which the applicant attends as a regular participant.

• Medical examination/evaluation is performed by the staff physician.

• Only the applicant's personal physician performs a functional assessment.

• Multidisciplinary intake and assessment team consists of a registered nurse, registered physical and speech therapists, a registered recreational therapist, a dietitian consultant, and a social worker.

• New participants receive a screening/assessment from a dentist, a podiatrist, and an ophthalmologist.

• Final decision on program admission is made by the applicant's personal physician and the backup medical panel of the affiliated health facility.

Participant Characteristics

Participants in these 10 adult day care programs are varied in their demographic and health characteristics. Several centers serve a particular racial or ethnic group. On Lok is a typical example; it serves a catchment area that is predominantly of one ethnicity, in this case Chinese.

Average age varies by program, too. While the average age for the 10 programs studied is 71, Burke has many participants younger than 60 and one participant, a paraplegic, who is only 22. At Burke, more than half the population is partially or totally paralyzed. At St. Camillus, just under half are similarly afflicted. At most other programs, paralyzed participants make up between a tenth and a third of the population. Wheelchair use is similarly heavily skewed. Three-quarters of the participants at St. Camillus and half those at Burke use a wheelchair all the time or some of the time.

Burke and St. Camillus also have the greatest number of participants suffering from fractures and strokes. Mental illness, the primary diagnosis of nearly three-fourths of the participants at St. Otto's, afflicts between a quarter and a third of participants in 5 of the 10 programs. Hypertension is a ubiquitous affliction among adult day care participants. Blindness is rare, yet at every program except St. Otto's and San Diego there is at least one blind participant.

Overall, the participants included in the sample tended to have between two and five diagnosed medical problems (see table 3.2).

Staffing and Health Care Services

Several programs depend on affiliated institutions to provide therapies. Others depend on in-house staff. Tucson has a large staff of

Table 3.2 Occurrence of Chronic Conditions and Impairments of Participants at Each of 10 Adult Day Care Programs (sample size for each program = 30)

Medical Problem	Athens No.	Athens Per-cent	Burke No.	Burke Per-cent	Levindale No.	Levindale Per-cent	Lexington No.	Lexington Per-cent
Angina	2	(7)	3	(10)	5	(17)	0	(–)
Myocardial Infarction	2	(7)	6	(20)	1	(3)	0	(–)
Cardiac Arrythmias	0	(–)	9	(30)	10	(33)	0	(13)
Congestive Heart Failure	3	(10)	8	(27)	8	(27)	12	(40)
Hypertension	13	(43)	21	(70)	13	(43)	15	(50)
Cerebrovascular Accident	6	(20)	14	(47)	3	(10)	6	(20)
Arteriosclerosis	10	(33)	19	(63)	3	(10)	14	(47)
Arthritis	15	(50)	9	(30)	7	(23)	10	(33)
Diabetes	7	(23)	7	(23)	9	(30)	9	(30)
Mental Illness	7	(23)	8	(27)	10	(33)	1	(3)
Neurologic								
Chronic Brain Syndrome	3	(10)	0	(–)	1	(3)	6	(20)
Mental Retardation	0	(–)	0	(–)	3	(10)	0	(–)
Parkinsonism	2	(7)	0	(–)	6	(20)	0	(–)
Other	1	(3)	6	(20)	4	(13)	3	(10)
Respiratory								
Emphysema	2	(7)	0	(–)	1	(3)	3	(10)
Other	1	(3)	1	(3)	0	(–)	4	(13)
Paralysis/Paresis	3	(10)	16	(53)	3	(10)	6	(20)
Fractures	4	(13)	6	(20)	1	(3)	1	(3)
Blindness	1	(3)	3	(10)	1	(3)	1	(3)
Average number of medical conditions per participant	2.7		4.8		2.9		3.3	

professional, allied, and associated health care personnel, but since it also has the largest population, it has, paradoxically, one of the proportionately smaller staffs. Burke has the highest ratio of staff to participants. St. Otto's eleven participants are served by the equivalent of fewer than three full-time staff members. The result overall is a range of nearly one staff member for every participant at Burke to just over one staff member for every five participants at St. Otto's.

Table 3.2 (continued)

Montefiore		On Lok		St. Camillus		St. Otto's		San Diego		Tucson	
No.	Per-cent	No.	Per-cent	No.	Per-cent	No.	Per-cent	No.	Per-cent	No.	Per-cent
7	(23)	2	(7)	1	(3)	2	(7)	2	(7)	0	(–)
3	(10)	0	(–)	1	(3)	2	(7)	0	(–)	4	(13)
4	(13)	5	(17)	4	(13)	1	(3)	3	(10)	3	(10)
7	(23)	9	(30)	2	(7)	1	(3)	0	(–)	1	(3)
13	(43)	12	(40)	12	(40)	6	(20)	13	(45)	13	(43)
4	(13)	12	(40)	10	(33)	1	(3)	6	(20)	10	(33)
19	(63)	18	(60)	6	(20)	3	(10)	7	(23)	9	(30)
17	(57)	10	(33)	8	(27)	3	(10)	7	(23)	9	(30)
8	(27)	8	(27)	2	(7)	0	(–)	3	(10)	7	(23)
11	(37)	6	(37)	4	(13)	21	(70)	2	(7)	9	(30)
4	(13)	5	(17)	0	(–)	4	(13)	5	(17)	3	(10)
0	(–)	0	(–)	0	(–)	6	(20)	1	(3)	0	(–)
1	(3)	2	(7)	1	(3)	1	(3)	2	(7)	0	(–)
2	(7)	1	(3)	8	(26)	2	(7)	1	(3)	0	(–)
0	(–)	6	(20)	6	(20)	1	(3)	1	(3)	0	(–)
1	(3)	1	(3)	2	(7)	1	(3)	0	(–)	2	(7)
3	(10)	9	(30)	13	(43)	1	(3)	6	(20)	10	(33)
4	(13)	3	(10)	8	(27)	1	(3)	4	(13)	4	(13)
1	(3)	1	(3)	1	(3)	0	(–)	0	(–)	1	(3)
3.9		3.5		3.0		2.0		2.1		3.0	

Services

Few aspects of adult day care better evidence its evolving nature than the heterogeneity of service packages. Every program offers a core of basic services without which it could not function. But the similarities end there. What is most indicative of the fledgling nature of the program is that there is no apparent agreement on what marginal services have priority. The following basic and marginal services are offered in numerous combinations.

Basic services offered by all programs:
- general nursing services,
- referral to community services including: emergency services at hospital, emergency services of physician, ambulance transportation, hospital inpatient care, rehabilitation center, mental health facility, senior citizens' center, nursing home, community health center, visiting nurse/homemaker service, health specialists/consultants,
- social work services,
- recreation activities,
- assistance with activities of daily living,
- supervision of personal hygiene,
- lunch.

Additional services offered by some programs:
- two meals a day,
- snacks,
- nutritional counseling,
- meals-on-wheels,
- physician services,
- speech, physical, and occupational therapy,
- psychiatric services,
- psychological services,
- limited diagnostic services,
- rehabilitative nursing,
- music therapy,
- reality therapy,
- health education,
- sheltered workshop,

- laundry,
- transportation,
- home care services.

Additional services offered by some programs (through an outside source):
- diabetic treatment and care,
- ophthalmology,
- podiatry services,
- dental services,
- specialized diagnostic services,
- vocational rehabilitation,
- radiology.

Costs

The wide variations among adult day care programs in their physical facilities, staff size, variety of health professionals, and available services may make some difference in their ability to serve different populations. But there can be no doubt that they make a difference in their costs.

Daily costs at Burke are much higher, for nearly every function, than at any other program (see table 3.3). In fact, costs are nearly twice as high there as at the next most costly programs ($21.04 per day). But with that exception, costs fall within a fairly narrow range.

Conclusions

The preceding data suggest several things about the nature of adult day care in the United States. First, adult day care may be a special mode of care in one important respect: Its characteristics change from one center to the next. Virtually no statement can be made about patient characteristics, services, staffing, or costs without at least one exception. Second, what the 10 centers studied have in common is that in most cases they are highly adaptive to the local health care delivery system and local aged population's needs. What is missing from that system can be found in the adult day care program; what is already available usually is not duplicated.

Table 3.3   Per Diem Costs in 10
Day Care Programs

Center	Cost
Burke	$61.56
Montefiore	33.67
St. Camillus	24.51
On Lok	23.45
Athens	21.70
San Diego	20.94
Tucson	20.32
Levindale	16.97
Lexington	16.56
St. Otto's	11.26
Average for all 10	$25.09
Average excluding Burke	$21.04

This finding more than any other may point to great promise for adult day care in the United States, because it hints that growing resistance to further proliferation of new health care facilities (e.g., certificate of need laws) will not be a barrier to the development of programs. Tailored as they are to gaps in the existing system and shunning duplication, they meet the optimal standards of health planners.

Yet this very strength could retard growth, at least temporarily, if the growing concern about health care quality standards forces local program planners to adopt a standardized program definition instead of focusing on designs specially tailored to local conditions and patient needs. Without such tailored programs, adult day care might price itself out of the market even if quality of life is improved. At more than $21 for a four-hour day, the day care program is more expensive than a nursing home program (which averages $16 per day according to DHEW's 1975 Nursing Home Survey) for anyone who comes more than a couple of days each week.

A third influence in the health care policy field may solve the problem, however. This is the tendency of some officials to opt for decentralization of control over health care resource expenditures, favoring state and local level decision making over national policies. Former President Ford's health proposals in his 1976 budget message were good examples. He proposed collapsing some 59 categorical health programs into one block grant to the states. This found little support in Congress, but the fact that it was proposed may indicate that some support exists for putting the power to design health programs into the hands of those close enough to local delivery systems to see gaps and work to fill them. No program could be better suited to such flexibility than adult day care. If decentralization catches on, adult day care has a good chance of catching on with it.

The national expansion of adult day care, however, is further complicated by the following:

1. Even though many facilities use the name, there is no nationally accepted definition or concept of geriatric day care centers.

2. There is no clear philosophy to guide health and social service components on long-term care.

3. There is no national funding mechanism for day care.

4. Despite much governmental and professional involvement in day care, many, if not the majority, of centers develop in isolation; only a few states have established guidelines for the creation of day care centers.

Until the national problems are resolved, however, new initiatives in the development of adult day care must continue to be taken on the state and local level.

Notes

1. William Weissert, "A Preliminary Directory of Adult Day Care Programs" (Rockville, Md.: National Center for Health Services Research, Health Resources Administration, Public Health Service, Department of Health, Education and Welfare, 1974).

2. Willaim Weissert, *Adult Day Care in the U.S.: A Comparative Study*, final report funded by contract #HRA–B6–74–148 (Rockville, Md.: National Center for Health Services Research, Health Resources Administration, Public Health Service, Department of Health, Education and Welfare, 1975).

3. Amitai Etzioni, "Nursing Homes: New Rules Are Not Enough," *The Washington Post*, May 25, 1975, p. C3.

4. Ibid.

5. *Background Information on Medical Expenditures, Prices and Costs* (Rockville, Md.: Office of Research and Statistics, Social Security Administration, Department of Health, Education and Welfare, September 1974), p. 62.

6. Ibid.

7. *Long-Term Care Facility Survey, Interim Report* (Rockville, Md.: Office of Nursing Home Affairs, Department of Health, Education and Welfare, March 4, 1975), p. 2.

8. Erwin Witkin, *The Impact of Medicare* (Springfield, Ill.: Charles C Thomas, 1971), p. 9.

9. Betty Reichert, "And the Walls Come Tumbling Down: Humanizing the Institutional Aspects of Long-Term Care," *Human Factors in Long-Term Health Care, Final Report of the Task Force* (Columbus, Oh.: National Conference on Social Welfare, June 1975), p. 63.

10. Ibid., p. 65.

11. *Nursing Home Care in the United States: Failure in Public Policy, Supporting Paper No. 1, The Litany of Nursing Home Abuses and an Examination of the Roots of Controversy* (Washington, D.C.: Subcommittee on Long-Term Care, Special Committee on Aging, U.S. Senate, December 1974).

12. *Long-Term Care Facility Improvement Study, Introductory Report* (Washington, D.C.: Office of Nursing Home Affairs, Department of Health, Education and Welfare, July 1975), p. 1.

13. Ibid.

14. *A Promise Kept* (Rockville, Md.: Health Resources Administration, Division of Long-Term Care, Department of Health, Education and Welfare, November 1975).

15. Brahna Trager, "The Community in Long-Term Care," *Human Factors in Long-Term Care, Final Report of the Task Force* (Columbus, Oh.: National Conference on Social Welfare, June 1975).

16. Jean M. Maxwell, *Centers for Older People* (Washington, D.C.: The National Council on Aging, 1973), p. 5.

17. Ibid.

18. Ibid.

19. Ibid., p. 8.

20. William Weissert, *Adult Day Care in the U.S.: A Comparative Study,* final report funded by contract #HRA–B6–74–148 (Rockville, Md.: National Center for Health Services Research, Health Resources Administration, Public Health Service, Department of Health, Education and Welfare, 1975).

Useful Readings

Developments in Aging: 1975 and January–May 1976, Part 1 and 2, A Report of the Special Committee on Aging, U.S. Senate (Washington, D.C.: U.S. Government Printing Office, June 26, 1976).

Directory of Adult Day Care Centers (Rockville, Maryland: Health Standards and Quality Bureau, Health Care Financing, Administration, Department of Health, Education and Welfare, September 1977).

"Reimbursement under Title XIX for Services to the Chronically Ill and Impaired in Alternative Settings," *Field Staff Information and Instruction Series: #139* (Washington, D.C.: Social and Rehabilitative Service, Department of Health, Education and Welfare, April 9, 1973).

4

Levindale and Lexington: Two Models of Service Delivery

Introduction

The Levindale and Lexington day care centers exemplify two distinct patterns of development. Levindale was established in an institutional setting; Lexington was developed as a free-standing center. The adaptability of the day care center concept is apparent in the history of these two centers. Although each center developed in a different setting, both were established to fill the serious gaps in long-term care services available to the elderly population.

Levindale Adult Day Treatment Center

An important factor in planning the Levindale Geriatric Day Care Center was the documentation of existing and projected needs of the community. Two separate but related projects were undertaken that provided the basic planning and information for the day care center. First was an in-depth evaluation by Dr. Cecil Shepps of New York, a consultant to the Associated Jewish Charities of Baltimore, of the current and future health care needs of the aged living in the community.[1] This report was accompanied by an evaluation of existing health care resources for the aged. The second effort was a 1969 sociodemographic survey of the Jewish community of Baltimore also funded by the Associated Jewish Charities of Baltimore.[2] This survey generated a special substudy of the sociodemographic characteristics of the aged. Each effort provided part of the information required for health service planning activities that were to occur throughout the next decade.

The Shepps report offered the views of a single expert in community and geriatric medicine. In it, each health and health-related service agency sponsored by the community was examined to determine the following: the range of current services provided by each agency; the service needs each agency was fulfilling for its client group; the capacity for service expansion given existing levels of resources; and the perceptions of each agency's key personnel about service mission, service effectiveness, and interservice agency relations. The report concluded that each agency was providing a high quality of service and that there was not much duplication of services. On the other hand, there were many gaps in the health care system because additional, more specialized services and better interagency coordination were needed.

The 1969 sociodemographic survey provided important descriptive information about the population, but it did not inquire about the functional capacity of the elderly, nor did it provide information about what services they wished to have made available to them under the auspices of the Jewish community. Two major findings from this survey were important to service planning. It provided a clearer understanding of the geographic distribution of the aged Jewish population throughout the northwest sector of Baltimore and showed that there were large numbers of older persons who continued to live in transitional urban areas (i.e., most lived in apartments or single family dwellings in neighborhoods with high concentrations of middle-class blacks and, therefore, this subgroup varied from the younger Jewish population). Furthermore, it showed that the incomes of a large proportion of the elderly were at or slightly above the poverty level. Despite financial eligibility, a significant number had not applied for Medicaid and resisted doing so. This data, combined with an analysis of Levindale's waiting list for inpatient admission, indicated the need for service alternatives for the marginally functioning aged, supplemented by a transportation system. Therefore, the executive director of Levindale decided to start a day care program to offer the marginally impaired access to supportive health and social services without forcing them to give up their homes.

Resources

When a day care center is part of an institutionally based program, it is usually housed in the institution itself. Therefore, Levindale's center was located in one of the major inpatient buildings. Planning a day care center in this patient care unit involved many different considerations, including space, equipment, staffing, programming, licensing, and funding.

Arranging for adequate space is very important and often involves difficult decisions, depending upon the amount available and the anticipated demands of programming. Purchase of equipment (e.g., furniture, and program/service items) was tailored according to available space and budgetary limitations. Space was a problem at Levindale but was maximized through utilization of existing inpatient treatment areas. However, as was repeatedly demonstrated in this program and others, the day care center must have some area it can call its own.

The staffing and programming component of Levindale's day care program reflects the uniqueness of an institutionally based day care center. In general, the more recreational, occupational, and physical facilities the sponsoring institution has available for inpatients, the more therapeutic services can be offered by the day care center staff. At Levindale this included a registered nurse, a professional social worker, and a nurse's aide. The administrative core of the institution was used as a resource for purchasing, billing, payroll, and administration. But it is essential that overall conduct and management of all day care program activities should rest in the hands of a single director working full time. It is also crucial for certain core activities to be solely for day care patients. A day care program that only uses the programs of the parent institution does not seem to function well.

The Levindale day care program is not an independently licensed program, but is covered under the licensure of the institution. The experimental status of this center and of programs in the state of Maryland has precluded the necessity for licensure and other such regulatory mechanisms. In the future, as day care programs become an established health service, licensure will be required. It is possible that different standards will be developed to correspond with the level and type of health care.

Originally the Levindale program was funded by a three-year

demonstration grant from the Maryland State Commission on Aging. In 1972, Levindale received a research grant from the Medical Services Administration/Administration on Aging that was used to establish an ongoing evaluation effort independent of the programmatic component. Funding for the center depends on reimbursement for participants who are eligible for Title XIX and on persons who are able to pay the full per-diem cost. A small number of participants receive financial assistance from community funds in the form of "program scholarships." At this time, the administration is exploring the possibility of additional funding from Title XX.

The Program

The program begun in July, 1970, was one of the first health-related day care centers in the United States. Though it provides health care, it places greater programmatic emphasis on social services. Participants receive an individualized treatment plan developed by an interdisciplinary team of day care staff members and subsequently reviewed at 12-week to 16-week intervals. Minor or major revisions are made depending upon the changing needs and circumstances of the individual. The program is summarized in Table 4.1.

Transportation deserves special attention because it is both a major need of the elderly and a major problem for day care programs. Without a solid transportation system, a geriatric day care center is not really viable. Furthermore, as most participants spend a significant amount of time traveling to and from the center, this time should be conceived as a part of the service. Several options should be explored: contracting for the full service with a for-profit or community-sponsored system, hiring part-time drivers for center-owned vehicles, hiring full-time personnel to handle transportation and other duties, and a combination of these.

Levindale's experience with transportation is not unlike that reported by other program administrators. The size of the program, level of impairment of participants, geographical boundaries of the target population, and projected attendance patterns were critical factors in the preliminary decision making. It was difficult to determine the most desirable type of vehicles and it was sometimes impossible to obtain enough funds to purchase them. Between 1970 and 1974, Levindale used a specially designed camper, a hydraulic-lift

Table 4.1 Staffing and Services Provided by Levindale Day Care Center

Health-Related	Social-Related	ADL*	Transportation
Medications[a]	Social casework[a]	Bathing[a]	To and from home[a]
Modified exercises[a]	Social group work[a]	Dietary[a]	Scheduled visits[a]
Dressings and treatments[a]	Arts and crafts[a]		
Chiropody[b]	Birthdays and celebrations[a]		
Occupational therapy[b]	Field trips[a]		
Physical therapy[b]	Movies[a]		
Speech therapy[b]	Reading sessions[a]		
Physical exams[c]	Religious activities[a]		
Psychiatric services[c]	Beauty shop[b]		
Physician services[c]	Sheltered workshop[b]		
	Music therapy[c]		
	Community group presentations[c]		

*ADL = Activities of daily living.
a = Provided directly by center staff.
b = Available through inpatient resources.
c = Community resources coordinated by center staff.

van, and a station wagon. Eventually, considerable funds were spent on specially designed school-minibuses adapted for wheelchair patients. These minibuses are still not completely satisfactory because of mechanical problems, but they are a vital equipment resource.

Availability of proper equipment does not insure a good transportation system. Daily scheduling for pickup and delivery of 30 to 35 persons is a time-consuming and often harassing task. The following problems have been present in Levindale's program since 1970 and have never been completely resolved: matching transportation boundaries with the geographic catchment, coordinating convenient times for 30 aged persons and their families, daily rescheduling to accommodate absenteeism, avoiding lengthy travel times for those picked up first and dropped off home last, securing reliable drivers at a reasonable cost, determining what additional transportation to other community services will be provided during the day (e.g., doctor and clinic visits), handling problems when vehicles are late or have mechanical failures while patients are aboard, using travel time for effective programming. Many of these transportation problems are accentuated for programs located in rural areas.

Objectives

The concept of a geriatric day care center at Levindale was implemented to fulfill the following service objectives:

1. to provide socialization experience to physically and emotionally disabled older people,

2. to help maintain disabled older people in their homes and communities,

3. to provide an integrated professional service to disabled people living in the community,

4. to provide support and relief to families caring for their older disabled relative.

Goal formulation involved five factors: evaluation of the service needs of applicants to the institution who were relegated to the waiting list, evaluation of gaps in community services to avoid duplication, compilation of reactions of professionals in the community who worked with the impaired aged, review of the project prospectus according to the long-term goals of the institution, and consultation with health and social experts not directly related to the institution.

Target Population

The target population of the center is defined by the broad admission criteria that have been applied quite consistently to applicant selection since 1971. Participants must:

1. be 65 years old or more and/or chronically impaired,

2. preferably be Jewish,

3. have a community physician,

4. have a stable living arrangement with a family member or surrogate who assumes responsibility for the person,

5. live within a six-mile radius for the use of transportation service,

6. be able to pay the full cost of the program, or apply for Medicaid if eligibility has not been previously determined,

7. not be bed-ridden (wheelchair-bound participants are accepted),

8. be able to communicate their need to staff (verbally or non-verbally),

9. not be chronic alcoholics or drug addicts,

10. not be potentially harmful to themselves or others,

11. be judged eligible for an intermediate level of care with potential for maintenance at the same functional level (rehabilitation potential may not necessarily be indicated),

12. have a physician's certification of eligibility to attend a minimum of three days per week.

Using the criteria of a six-mile radius and 55 years of age, the census tract information indicates approximately 4,000 Jewish people. Assuming that five percent of them need institutional care, the estimate is that at any given time 120 persons are eligible and/or in need of the day care services. With an average of 30 participants at any given time, the program is now satisfying one quarter of the need.

During the first three years of operation, a sliding fee scale permitted flexible financial requirements. This was possible because the day care center was supported under the three-year grant from the State Commission on Aging. With the advent of Medicaid reimbursement and the termination of the grant, more rigid financial criteria were established and more consistently applied. The religious criterion does not preclude processing members of other religious groups for intake, but only an insignificant minority of clients have been of other religious faiths.

It should be noted that in the fifteen day care centers surveyed by Levindale in a 1974 preliminary survey[3] the two most common admission characteristics found are also the most common for Levindale: the ability of a family member or surrogate to assume responsibility for the individual during non-day care hours and a physician in the community who provides the medical care.

Intake and Utilization Procedures

The intake procedures have many steps. First is the inquiry by the elderly person, a family member, or a professional person on behalf of the applicant. Inquiries may or may not lead to the second stage, which is an interview with the social worker and the family unit at the center. Initial telephone interviews give the social worker an opportunity to summarize the services provided at the center and to determine the immediate perceived needs of the aged person and/ or the family. An initial face-to-face interview is strongly encouraged at the end of the phone interview because it provides the social worker with an opportunity to make a fairly comprehensive evaluation of the appropriateness of the service. During the second interview the aged person is required to join with family members at the center to observe the program and be observed by the social worker and the nurse coordinator. The final stage of intake is an interdisciplinary assessment by the social worker and the nurse coordinator through which the final intake decision is reached.

As a result of Medicaid reimbursement regulations, the staff is exploring the possibility of modifying the utilization review procedures applied to the Medicaid inpatients at Levindale. It has been determined that this review method will increase the program's conformity with Medicaid inpatient care regulations and provide a systematic method for ongoing participant assessment.

Conclusions and Summary

The Levindale experience highlights important aspects of planning and program implementation in institutionally based geriatric day care centers. It is clear that the institutional setting has an impact on the delivery of day care services. However, the Levindale geriatric day care center also influences the parent organization. Integration between the institution and other community services has increased. The traditional image of Levindale as an old age home has been changed. A wider range of service resources have been offered to persons seeking long-term care. The importance of the family in the delivery of long-term care has been underscored. The local and national reputation of the institution as an innovative long-term care organization has been enhanced.

On the other hand, the center has had some negative impact on the institution. It has taxed the administrative staff to its fullest to provide the necessary leadership, created a need for much inservice education to help orient staff to the goals and objectives of the day care center, forced staff to work toward integration of inpatients and day care participants, and forced the institution into an ongoing struggle over program funds. The vital aspects of program funding represent the single major administrative dilemma. In Levindale's case, it was necessary to spend months negotiating with state Medicaid authorities to prove the validity of day care services as an alternative to inpatient care and then to work toward a reimbursement policy. This interrelationship continues to present problems in processing applicants for Medicaid reimbursement as well as in handling periodic renegotiations of the level of reimbursement.

Lexington Centers for Creative Living

The Lexington-Fayette County Health Department is a public health agency charged with the responsibility for implementing state and local public health laws. It serves the community of approximately 210,000 residents of Lexington-Fayette County, which is a merged city-county municipality. Initially, programs were limited to traditional public health programs, but the need for improved and expanded programs in the area of long-term care in the community became evident to health department officials. A serious gap existed between homebound care provided by the local home health agency and care in the 24-hour institutional setting. Through its nursing home inspection program and home health agency services, the department could readily identify aged persons who were at risk or in the process of being institutionalized inappropriately because of the lack of community support services.

Conversations among the community's Council on Aging, local and state welfare agencies, and employees of the health department's geriatric programs resulted in the development of the day center concept. Reaction to this concept was extremely positive, and leaders of programs for the aged and of health programs encouraged development. State and local welfare agencies were able to identify clients whom they believed would benefit from the service. Individuals responsible for institutional care saw this service as a means of helping to reduce the growing waiting lists for the community's nursing homes and especially for helping lower-income patients, who were dependent upon the state's Medicaid program.

In order to assess the target population, estimate the persons at risk, and gauge patient interest in a day center program, the health department conducted a health status survey of the community's elderly.[4] A list of public assistance recipients was obtained from the state public assistance agency and, with the cooperation of the University of Kentucky College of Nursing, an interview schedule was arranged. The Intake, Periodic, and Discharge Questionnaire was the instrument used to evaluate the functional levels of the participants, and items were included that assessed the participants' interest in attending an adult day care program. Two hundred and fifty interviews were conducted during the survey period. Fifty-two people (approximately 20 percent) were identified as needing adult day care intervention and indicated a willingness to participate in such a program. This initial survey proved invaluable when the first day care center opened in May, 1973, as the first 12 participants were among these interested individuals.

During the second year of operation of the first center the waiting list became quite unmanageable—over 60 applicants—so the health department decided to establish a second adult day care center. The center had been approached by representatives of a local Episcopal Church, and an arrangement was made with the church to occupy space in a building owned and operated by them. Consequently, in February, 1975, a second Center for Creative Living was opened in Lexington. Again, financial support was provided through private organizations. The Kentucky Social Welfare Foundation contributed money for the initial expenses, the Junior League assisted in getting equipment donated for use at the center, and the Altrusa Club, a local civic organization, donated some funds for operating expenses.

Shortly after the first adult day care center opened, there was much discussion about the name and the negative implications of "adult day care." It was decided to let the participants at the center decide on a name. They unanimously decided on "Center for Creative Living," which has been used ever since. This name seems very adequately to embody the founding concepts of the program and the feelings of its participants.

Resources

Potential funding sources in the community were identified and contacted. After testing the idea of an adult day care program, a written plan was developed to present to potential funding sources. This plan included an explanation of the concept and identified the major objectives of the center. It also detailed the resources needed to operate the program.

The community was canvassed to determine which agencies and groups were interested in sponsoring the project. A critical concern in this process was with private funds. It was believed that if a private community club or group that had an interest in such a project could be identified, there would be a great deal more community support. The Junior League of Lexington decided to sponsor the project, an important step in the development of the Lexington center.

The Junior League of Lexington provided $36,000 to help the day care center get underway. In addition, the local community mental health center, which was very concerned about improved services to the aged, provided $10,000 for staffing the program. Encouraged by these initial contributors, the health department sought additional financial assistance from the local Council on Aging. With the contributed funds, the Lexington-Fayette County Health Department developed a proposal that was approved and accepted for funding through Title III of the Older Americans Act. This grant not only provided funding for the development of the center, but also included $3,000 for evaluating the cost and effectiveness of the services.

During the second year, Title III funds were no longer available, so the program had to develop an alternative funding agency. A contract was initiated with the Kentucky Department for Human Resources to provide services through Title VI of the Social Security Act. In addition to this source, the center also received waivers of the present Medicare and Medicaid guidelines to obtain reimbursement for participants accepted for a long-term research and demonstration project sponsored by DHEW. A sliding fee scale was set for participants who did not qualify for any of the programs.

Although no licensure requirements were in effect at the time the adult day care center was developed, under health planning laws in effect in 1973, any new health service was required to obtain a certificate of need. Data obtained through the health status survey were extremely helpful in documenting the need for the center. It was estimated that at least two percent of the community's 20,000 elderly could benefit from the services. On this basis, the certificate of need was granted to the health department.

The Lexington center differed from most of the day care programs in existence at the time because it was to be in a free-standing, noninstitutionally based facility. This made many of the organizational relationships more complex than they were for the institutionally based centers. For example, therapeutic services such as podiatry and ophthalmology would be provided in the practitioner's office rather than in the facility. Also, having some therapists visit the facility created scheduling problems and difficulties in coordinating services.

A critical factor in the success of the Lexington Centers for Creative Living has been the strong support of the health department, which assumed the major responsibility for developing the original plan and introducing the concept to the health providers and community. Community support also has been crucial to success. Early and continued involvement of the community has always received strong emphasis. A citizens' advisory council for the centers was established when the first center opened. It is composed of 20 people from all professions interested in problems of the aged. The council has given invaluable advice and resources to the program.

Center for Creative Living I is housed in a historic mansion that was donated to the city of Lexington as a recreational facility. It has been adapted to the center's activity, treatment, dining, and office space needs. Center for Creative Living II is housed in an old water company building owned by Christ Episcopal Church. This building has served the program well because of private treatment areas and adequate personal care space.

The Program

The Centers for Creative Living provide a variety of health and social services to the participants. These services are provided five days a week, and begin each day at 9:00 A.M., when patients first arrive. The day is structured to integrate the medical care into a matrix of social activities and special therapies:

1. *Multiphasic screening* is provided for tuberculosis, diabetes, visual and hearing defects, podiatric and dental problems.

2. *Nursing care* is provided by a registered nurse with the assistance of health service aides. This care includes dispensation of medication, catheter care, application of dressings and compresses, assistance with and teaching of personal hygiene, and counseling participants and their families. The registered nurse also coordinates medical care with the participant's family physician in developing care plans, administering special treatments, and performing specified laboratory work-ups, e.g., blood samples, cultures, and specimens.

3. *Recreational and occupational therapy services* are designed to improve, maintain, and stimulate physical, mental, and social functioning. Those who are able to participate actively take walks, play croquet and badminton, and take part in other outdoor activities. Indoor activities include games, group singing, guest entertainment, community visits to shopping centers and other public facilities, group discussions, and a variety of crafts. A number of community volunteers donate many hours for some of the activity programs.

4. *Medical care and supervision* are provided under the direction of the participant's attending physician. In addition, dental, podiatric, and ophthalmologic care are offered to all participants through personal service contracts with the appropriate providers in the community.

5. *Physical therapy* is provided by a licensed physical therapist, who is employed on a part-time contractual basis. The therapist evaluates all new participants, and develops and supervises a plan of care that is implemented by a trained health service aide.

6. *Social service* is provided by a social worker with a baccalaureate degree and supervised by a social worker with a master's degree. Regular attendance at the center and participation in its numerous activities provide a variety of socialization opportunities. Remotivation and reality therapy are offered in addition to family and individual counseling.

7. *Speech therapy* is offered by a licensed speech therapist. The therapist also teaches aides how to reinforce treatment on those days when a session is not held with the speech therapist.

At each center, the services listed above are provided by a registered nurse assisted by the following staff: one social worker, one recreational therapist, three health service aides, one food service aide, two part-time bus drivers, one consulting occupational therapist (who provides some direct care at both centers), and one clerk for both centers. Contracts cover physical therapy, speech therapy, and ophthalomogic, dental, podiatric, and psychiatric care.

Participants usually leave the center at 3:30 P.M. Most are transported by the center's four vans, two of which are equipped with hydraulic lifts for wheelchair participants. Transportation also is offered during the day for physician and various medical appointments.

Objectives

In order to evaluate the center's services, it was hypothesized that the program could offer a viable alternative to institutionalization and prevent many unnecessary institutional placements. Specifically, the center formulated the following objectives:

1. The majority of the Center for Creative Living participants would improve or be maintained on their physical, social, emotional, and medical levels of functioning.

2. The majority of participants would show increased independence in their daily lives.

3. The majority of participants would be deterred from premature or total institutionalization.

4. Those participants who had a history of dysfunctional family relationships prior to entering the program would experience a lessening of family tensions and conflicts.

5. Family members who had the responsibility of 24-hour care prior to the day care service would experience a greater amount of free time to pursue employment opportunities or leisure time activities.

It was also believed that the center would have an impact on the community. Not only would it provide an additional health care option in the service delivery network, it would also encourage other community agencies to utilize and develop alternatives to institutional care. It was hoped that the center would demonstrate that the social/health model was an effective method of providing long-term

61

care services, and that the model would give rise to better total patient care planning, leading to more coordination among professional staff in medical and social agencies.

Target Population

The target population of the centers is defined by the broad admission criteria applied to the applicant selection process.

1. Applicants must be 55 years old or more. However, in special instances, applicants younger than 55 may be admitted with the approval of the center's Advisory Council and with documented needs.

2. All applicants must reside in Fayette County if they need and desire transportation. Applicants outside of the service area may attend if they supply their own transportation.

3. As a rule, patients are not admitted who have a gross psychiatric disability. Most patients who have had two or more psychiatric hospitalizations and are psychotic are not admitted.

4. At the time of referral, all applicants are interviewed and the Intake, Periodic, and Discharge Questionnaire (IPDQ) is administered. This questionnaire is designed to assess participants' functional abilities in the following areas: medical, physical, social, emotional, and daily life. The questionnaire was developed by the staff of the Lexington health department (see appendix A).

Intake and Utilization/Review Procedures

An important component of the day care program is the Intake and Utilization/Review Committee. This committee's primary purpose is to evaluate and admit all new participants and to reevaluate their progress regularly throughout their involvement in the program.

The intake questionnaires (IPDQ) developed by the health department staff assist the committee in making a decision regarding admission. The questionnaire is quantified; a numerical score is derived indicating the severity of need. Although this questionnaire does not always thoroughly evaluate an applicant's total functioning, it is a reasonable indicator of those who need the program.

The Intake and Utilization/Review Committee is interdisciplinary, with one or more representatives from the medical, nursing, and social work professions. Although other professionals may be included, it is essential that these three professions be the core of the committee. It is also helpful if one of the members has a mental health orientation or background.

Frequency and duration of meetings depends on the size of the day center and the number of participants attending. The Centers for Creative Living accommodate over 30 people each, and the committee holds meetings on a biweekly basis.

Probably the most important function of the committee is the periodic review of the participants' utilization of services. This is done on a rotating basis, with each participant being reviewed at least every three months. These reviews are formal presentations prepared by the day center staff. The major categories that should be considered are: primary and secondary diagnoses, status of the participant at the time of admission, reason for referral, course of treatment, and attendance. A form has been developed for this procedure (see appendix B).

After reviewing this data, the committee determines the priority status of each case and evaluates the present prescribed treatment days. Since the majority of participants initially attend five days per week, they often progress substantially and may need a reduction in the number of days they attend. The committee recommends any reductions it feels need to be made. If participants are attending poorly, the committee may review the problems and suggest approaches to increase the attendance rate. Utilization/Review can also plan treatment, and committee members often make recommendations regarding the alternatives that should be considered by the center's staff.

Conclusions and Summary

The success of the Centers for Creative Living can be attributed to the many links and relationships the agency maintains in the community. The program's policy-making advisory council and its volunteer program involve members of the Retired Senior Volunteer Program, University of Kentucky students, and other interested persons. A civic organization sponsors fund-raising projects to help purchase such special equipment as lifts for participants confined to wheelchairs.

The clergy is also active in the centers' activities and provides group religious services and individual pastoral counseling. The Society for the Blind offers special training and equipment for those who have lost their sight. The Department of Libraries shares films and brings its Bookmobile to the centers so participants may read current periodicals and check out books. The participants also take part in community bazaars and sell the arts and crafts they have made.

Of course, referral sources are a major part of the centers' interagency relationships. The centers receive referrals from all five Lexington hospitals. Private physicians refer people they see on an outpatient basis. The community mental health centers, the Bureau for Social Services, and the local Home Health Agency are sources of innumerable referrals.

The Centers for Creative Living were founded on sound planning, community support, and strong backing by the sponsoring agency. Their developmental history indicates that planners must examine the health and social problems of their particular community, identify the causes of the problems, document the need, mobilize community support, and seek a funding source. Experience shows that funding should be sought from several sources, including federal, state, and local governments, and the private sector.

Notes

1. Cecil Shepps, "Consultation Report on Future Geriatric Service Needs," consultation report prepared for the Associated Jewish Charities of Baltimore (Baltimore, Maryland, 1967).

2. Sidney Hollander Associates, "A Demographic Survey of the Jewish Community," consultation survey completed by Hollander Associates for the Associated Jewish Charities of Baltimore (Baltimore, Maryland, 1969).

3. *Preliminary Analysis of Select Geriatric Day Care Programs* (Washington, D.C.: Division of Long Term Care, Health Resources Administration, National Center for Health Services Research, Department of Health, Education, and Welfare, June 1974).

4. *Application for Project Grant under Title III of the Older Americans Act, Adult Day Care Center* (Lexington, Kentucky: Lexington-Fayette County Health Department, April 1973).

5

The Nursing Service
and the Role
of Nurse Coordinator

Introduction

Two major nursing functions are an essential part of health care in a geriatric day care setting. These functions are carried out in both the Lexington and Levindale centers and are presented here within the broader context of adult day care service delivery.

The first is the provision of direct nursing care: the nurse is directly involved with health problems of individuals and groups of individuals. The second function, nursing coordination, involves the nurse as part of a multidisciplinary health care team that shares responsibility for implementing the broader goals of adult day care. The nurse coordinator must have the ability to participate in health care as a collaborative effort, and to assume administrative and leadership responsibilities.

Both functions require the nurse to have expertise in geriatric nursing and the ability to engage in interdisciplinary communications and a diverse array of interactions with participants, families, and other day care staff. Competent performance of both functions is essential for effective health care delivery. These functions may be performed independently or concurrently, but both require a registered professional nurse. Although in this chapter selected functions are described separately, it is important to keep in mind that these functions may overlap.

The Geriatric Nurse

Geriatric nursing as a specialty is now receiving an increasing amount of interest and attention within the profession and from other health professionals. Almost every nursing journal has recently published an article related to the geriatric patient; a new journal of geriatric nursing—*The Journal of Gerontological Nursing*—is now available and subscribed to by many professionals. The American Nurses' Association has developed standards for geriatric nursing practice and established a Division of Geriatric Nursing Practice. These trends are representative of a significant movement to upgrade the quality of geriatric nursing care now practiced in varied settings.

Long-term care has traditionally been rendered in a manner that tends to homogenize the needs of the aging population. The aged have not been cared for as individuals, and personal values, styles of life, and other unique characteristics have been ignored. The geriatric nurse must be an expert on the aging process, have a special empathy with elderly persons, and have an ability to utilize knowledge and theories from diverse fields, including gerontology, sociology, psychology, medical science, and physiology. The nurse must be able to discriminate between that style of living which is usual and beneficial and that which can be dangerous. The person's right to independence must be weighed and considered in light of potential pathologic effects.

The geriatric nurse must recognize the value of the physical and psychosocial environment as a therapeutic tool and must, together with the older person, assist with changing and adapting it as needed within limitations imposed by the situation. For example, oftentimes a physical dimension of the home setting (e.g., sharing a bedroom or spending much time isolated from other family members) has a dysfunctional impact on the patient. The space barriers have psychosocial consequences that impede the person's participation in constructive activity and meaningful social exchange. These two factors not only interact with each other, but can have a significant role in the outcome of the nursing plan.

Perhaps the most unique feature of the adult day care center participant is the fact that he or she is at home or outside an institution at night and on the weekends. This has tremendous implications for the health professionals involved in planning and implementing the care plan because the potential for remaining an integral part of the family must be supported. Programs are designed to keep people living at home by providing organized care during the day. The living arrangements must be established and stabilized to enhance the likelihood of maintaining a participant in the center.

Direct Nursing Care at the Center

Direct nursing care involves assessment, problem identification, development of an appropriate plan, intervention or implementation of the proposed plan, and continuous evaluation.

The objective of service is to restore or maintain functions at a level of independence commensurate with capabilities. Since the services required to produce this kind of functional outcome are interdisciplinary, and nursing care must be coordinated with medical and social treatments, it is imperative that professionals from all the disciplines involved plan jointly to meet the needs of the adult day care participant.

All too often, some of the most important members of the planning team—patients and their families—are overlooked. No one knows better than they their goals, resources, desires, and limitations. It is not difficult to recognize the value of a patient's and family's cooperation in a treatment plan. How better to assure this cooperation than to include them in all levels of problem identification and planning?

The nurse has the unique opportunity of observing the patient over a prolonged period, but this frequency and closeness of contact can sometimes result in a dulling of the nurse's observational acuity, which can lead to oversights of obvious and not-so-obvious signs and symptoms. The nurse, therefore, must guard against this problem.

The first step in the provision of direct nursing care is assessment. Assessment may be defined as a "continuous, systematic, critical, orderly, and precise method of collecting, validating, analyzing, and interpreting information about the physical, psychological, and social needs of a patient and his family, the nature of the patient's self-care deficits, and other factors influencing his condition and care."[1]

Initial assessment of a day care participant should be done at intake to establish a data base on which to plan care. It should emphasize functional abilities and limitations based on data gathered from many sources. Direct observation and interviewing of patients and families are the methods most frequently used by nurses. Other methods include acquisition and study of written records, survey of the home and neighborhood, and discussions with other personnel who know the patient.

Direct observation and interviewing of patients is a complex process involving many facets of interpersonal relationships and communications. The nurse should strive for skill in this process. Attention to privacy and the participant's comfortable feeling as well as to the phrasing of questions and comments can assist in eliciting the information one would like to obtain. A nonjudgmental attitude is essential. It is also crucial to validate observations with the patient and family. Alertness to nonverbal communication can prove invaluable.

Answers to questions that provide information about the physical and psychological status of the patient are important. Standardized questions and scales are available from a diverse set of instruments. Some of these used in day care programs include: Patient Status Instrument,[2] Measurement of Life Satisfaction,[3] Physical and Mental Impairment of Function Evaluation in the Aged (PAMIE Scale),[4] and the Older Americans Resource Service Project Functional Rating Scales.[5]

Some of the generic questions used for information gathering follow:

Physical Health Status:
1. What are the primary diagnoses or health problems?
2. What are the current activity limitations?
3. What activities of daily living (e.g., feeding and bathing) and what instrumental activities of daily living (e.g., telephone, housecleaning) can be performed independently or need assistance?
4. What are the general health practices (e.g., smoking, drinking, and dietary)?

Mental Orientation Status:

1. Is the person oriented to time, person, and place consistently or periodically?

2. What is the attention span?

3. Is there a history of mental illness, retardation, or learning disability?

Depending on the availability of other professionals to participate in the initial assessment, the nurse may find it necessary to conduct a modified social service history. If necessary, the nurse should consult with professionals on the center's staff about what information items are most relevant for a psychosocial assessment.

A complete physical examination of the participant and a review of body systems can provide valuable baseline data and will require that the nurse develop additional skills in the use of such instruments as stethoscope, ophthalmoscope, and otoscope, as well as adeptness in palpation and percussion. With this information, the nurse is able to begin delineation of problems. A problem may be defined as any sign, symptom, act, response, or reaction observed in or cited by the patient requiring assistance from any member of the health team for the patient to regain and maintain his physical and psychosocial functioning.

Formulation of a care plan is another important nursing responsibility. A care plan must include specification of short-term and long-term goals. To be most easily measured, goals should be stated in terms of expected patient behaviors. Some examples of these are: The patient will walk with the aid of equipment within three months; the patient will become independent in toileting within eight weeks; the patient will, using aseptic techniques, be able to administer insulin injections within four weeks; the patient will have an increased number of social contacts at home within eight weeks. To implement these objectives, the nursing plan must include appropriate intervention.

If patient goals are stated behaviorally, there will be no problem in measuring whether or not they are met. For example, if the patient was to administer insulin injections using aseptic techniques, and this goal has not been met, it is necessary to review each of the component behaviors and procedures to determine possible causes. Assessment: Was a visual or learning impairment overlooked? Is his or her manual dexterity sufficient? Was he or she ready and willing to learn? Problem identification: Was the problem identified correctly? Planning: Were goals and approaches appropriate? Implementation: Was teaching individualized, meaningful, and implemented in a gradual, continuous way? Was sufficient time allowed for demonstration and practice? Was the equipment used while teaching? Was the atmosphere conducive to learning?

The nurse should not be self-berating when goals are not met, but should ascertain the reasons. We are all subject to error and should be willing to admit when we have erred in assessment or judgment. However, sometimes there are extenuating factors that have an influence on goal attainment, and the nurse must be aware of these and adapt or change them as appropriate. Such obvious factors as adequate equipment, space, and staff can have a real impact on the ability to deliver effective nursing care.

Successful intervention requires appropriate delegation. The appropriateness of delegation may vary, but a primary consideration is that the person to whom care responsibilities will be delegated must have the knowledge and skills to perform them and must receive ongoing education and supervision by the nurse. In general, the routine collection of data (e.g., temperature, pulse, respiration, blood pressure, and weight), selected physical treatments, and uncomplicated personal care may be delegated appropriately to less-skilled personnel. It has been reported that centers vary widely in the extent and pattern of delegation.[6] It is not appropriate to delegate those activities that require the observational skills and knowledge of the registered nurse, such as complex treatments or monitoring medications and their side effects.

Patient care planning is not effective unless it is an ongoing process. When it is static and based entirely on initial assessments, planning becomes an effort in futility. Reassessment and regular plan revision are crucial components in the provision of comprehensive, individualized nursing care.

Nursing Coordination

The nurse coordinator role involves the nurse as part of a multidisciplinary health care team that shares responsibility for implementing the broader goals of adult day care. The nurse coordinator has the administrative responsibilities in assuring that the expertise and collaboration of the adult day care team is brought to bear on a patient's health problems at the most effective time in order to provide optimum delivery and continuity of care.

Guiding the planning process is an important nursing role. This may be accomplished by scheduling regular planning or case-conference meetings of representatives from all disciplines involved in the patient's care. All disciplinary assessments should be completed before the conference so the session may be devoted to delineation of problems and development of plans and approaches. Case selection for each planning session should include newly admitted participants and participants being considered for discharge.

The nurse has a primary role in case coordination. The four-way interaction of family, physician, patient, and nurse is the most desirable for delivering health care in a geriatric day care center.[7] The experiences of the Lexington-Fayette County Health Department and the Levindale Hebrew Geriatric Center and Hospital suggest that the nurse plays a pivotal role in coordinating communication among patient, family, center staff, and physician. This function is even more crucial when physicians in the community provide medical supervision and care for their patients who participate in the center. The nurse can establish patterns of open communication by sharing information with both the physician and family.

The nurse assists the patient with the physician's medical regimen or the application and execution of physician's orders. This may involve administering medications, performing prescribed treatments, or assisting with diagnostic services. Certainly, an important consideration here is the communication and understanding between patient and physician. The nurse can be of real value in interpreting the physician's plans to the patient, as needed and appropriate. This function assumes even more importance when one realizes that the patient is not available for nursing supervision 24 hours a day, and must understand and be prepared to carry out safely and effectively the physician's plan of care during those times when he or she is away from the adult day health center.

The nurse should assume responsibility for guiding the development of, updating, and maintaining orderly record-keeping systems. All health-related information considered important for nursing care should be reviewed by the nurse, and outdated information removed from the records. The nurse should be familiar with the most current methods of problem-oriented record keeping, and should help to train other staff in the effective use of these modern methods.

The nurse coordinator assists in scheduling and obtaining input from the various professionals of the health care team. This function may be the most important in terms of providing comprehensive, well-planned, and effectively implemented care for each participant. It is critical that a mechanism be set up whereby each participant is assured multidisciplinary assessment and ongoing care and evaluation.

The scheduling problems related to getting participants to the right place at the right time are tremendous. Just getting participants to the center can be a real challenge in terms of scheduling pick-up routes and revising routes to account for absences and bus malfunctions. There are many potentially conflicting activities into which patients must be scheduled. Private physician or clinic appointments must be arranged and met. People must be notified and appointments canceled when participants are absent. Scheduling, needless to say, is a critical issue.

The nurse working in an adult day care setting is in a crucial spot to provide real assistance to elderly persons requiring additional community resources and should, therefore, be familiar with local community health and social resources.

Providing for care during emergencies is also the nurse coordinator's responsibility. The nurse coordinator must plan for emergency care during health crises. Protocols should be developed for reactions to drugs, anaphylactic shock, diabetic coma or insulin shock, first aid, and other expectable problems. Emergency equipment and supplies must be available. All staff should know how to perform cardiopulmonary resuscitation and what steps to take in a medical emergency.

One of the greatest threats to the aged is accidents. The safety component of the day care environment, therefore, is especially important because the hazards attendant on normal aging are compounded by illness and debility. The nurse coordinator has responsibility for the prevention of accidents in the center and should be aware of any potential hazards. The following criteria should be helpful in evaluating the environment:

1. There must be no irregularities in floors or thresholds.
2. Doors must be wide enough to accommodate wheelchairs and walkers.
3. Stairs, if present, must be well lighted and painted.
4. Handrails must be present in halls and stairs.
5. Rooms must be arranged to promote easy flow of traffic.
6. Lighting must be adequate.
7. Furniture must not have casters or sharp corners.
8. The environment must be uncluttered.
9. Scatter rugs must not be used.
10. Nonskid wax must be used.
11. Toilet facilities must be of suitable height, with grab bars and benches.
12. Exits must be well marked.
13. Carpets, draperies, and furniture must be as nonflammable as possible.

Representation of the day care center to the community may be part of the coordinator's role, particularly in the areas of volunteers and advisory committees. Recruitment, orientation, training, and scheduling of volunteers is a function through which the center can reap great benefits, since volunteers involve the community with the center and extend staff capabilities. Advisory committees can provide valuable input on program and policy issues; the nurse coordinator must assist in obtaining this input.

In conducting coordination functions, the nurse must employ administrative and management skill. Staffing is a crucial administrative task, and the nurse should help determine the size of staff, the balance of personnel, and criteria for selecting personnel. In making these decisions, the nurse should analyze the range of patient disability and the amount of community and home-support activities required. Job descriptions, which provide a guide for supervising other personnel, should not be prepared without major input from the nurse.

Conclusions

The nurse in an adult day care setting performs the same functions as geriatric nurses in other settings, but in some ways those functions are unique and expanded because she is part of an interdisciplinary team. This requires a different orientation. The nurse must think in terms of close collaboration with others and of integrating the nursing plan and nursing care into a total, effective whole. The nurse must increase triage functions and, therefore, must be more adept and skillful in observing signs, symptoms, and physical conditions that signal a change in health status.

There is an integration of the traditional roles of hospital nurse and home health nurse into day care nurse. Some of the coordination activities of the "head nurse" are present as well as the direct care component of home health nursing.

The adult day care nurse must accept responsibility for and be competent to perform as "core care" planner. The nurse must assume great responsibility and be comfortable in generating health care plans rather than passively implementing physician's orders. Many times the decisions regarding referrals and input from other disciplines rest with the nurse. The nurse must also monitor implementation of these services. The nurse in adult day care, therefore, must possess additional skills and knowledge that allow the translation of nursing needs into language meaningful to other professionals, and must understand the basics of other therapies to determine whether or not they are needed.

The nurse assumes an expanded role in the admission and discharge processes of an adult day care center. Traditionally, decisions regarding admission to or discharge from a health care facility have been the sole responsibility of the physician. The decisions regarding admission and discharge for adult day care, however, are joint, multidisciplinary processes.

Because, in most instances, participants will be living at home, either alone or with family, the nurse must plan additionally to meet the patient's nursing needs during those times when he or she is not at the center. This may involve the use of special teaching/learning sessions with the participant and the cooperation of family members, neighbors, friends, or community resources.

The nurse is in a pivotal position to enhance communication among patient, family, physician, and center staff. It is critical to the success of a patient's management and the center program as a whole that there be close collaboration in development and communication of a treatment plan.

Notes

1. Deane B. Taylor, *Systematic Nursing Assessment: A Step Toward Automation* (Washington, D.C.: U. S. Government Printing Office, Department of Health, Education and Welfare, No. HRA–74–17), p. 9.

2. Sidney Katz et al., "Progress in Development of the Index of ADL," *The Gerontologist,* part 1, Spring 1970, pp. 20–30; Sidney Katz et al., "Studies of Illness in the Aged; The Index of ADL: A Standardized Measure of Biological and Psychosocial Function," *Journal of the American Medical Association,* vol. 185, 1963, pp. 914–919.

3. Bernice Neugarten, Robert Havighurst, and Sheldon Tobin, "The Measurement of Life Satisfaction," *Journal of Gerontology,* vol. 16, 1961, pp. 134–143.

4. Lee Gurel, Margaret Linn, and Bernard S. Linn, "Physical and Mental Impairment of Function Evaluation in the Aged: The PAMIE Scale," *Journal of Gerontology,* vol. 27, no. 1, 1972, pp. 83–90.

5. Eric Pfeiffer et al., *Research Instrumentation for the Older American Resource Service Projects* (Durham, N.C.: Duke University, 1974).

6. Willuiam Weissert, *Adult Day Care in the U. S.: A Comparative Study,* final report funded by contract #HRA–B6–74–148 (Rockville, Md.: National Center for Health Services Research, Health Resources Administration, Public Health Service, Department of Health, Education and Welfare, 1975).

7. Eloise Rathbone-McCuan and Julia Levenson, "Geriatric Day Care Centers as an Open System Approach to Geriatric Health Care," paper presented at the 26th Annual Scientific Meeting of the Gerontological Society, Miami, Fla., November 1972.

6

Medical Care and Patterns of Provision

Introduction

Long-term care traditionally has not been one of the primary interests of physicians and health professionals. Medical education has been geared to the acutely ill in a hospital setting and there are few training programs for health professionals that emphasize chronic illness or the needs of the aged.[1] Furthermore, little teaching occurs in settings outside the acute care hospital. One has been lead to equate medicine with acute care hospitals; all else has been relegated to secondary status and importance. This situation, however, is beginning to change because of the increasing demands of the elderly in increasing numbers and with greater advocacy (e.g., Gray Panthers), and because of attempts by professionals to correct the obvious deficiencies in the present system. The physician, in particular, needs to become increasingly involved in long-term care because his role is pivotal in the system. Federal legislation is already promoting this involvement in some cases, for example, by requiring medical directors for nursing homes. These requirements, however, will not succeed unless there is a reevaluation of the needs of the chronically ill by the medical profession and a recognition of the differences between chronic and acute illness.

Special Components of Long-Term Care

There are several special components of long-term care that are of particular importance to the geriatric practitioner or the physician working with geriatric patients. These include the following:

Accurate diagnosis: Skilled medical examination and appropriate investigation are required. Common medical problems of the elderly center around the coexistence of many disorders or diseases and the predominance of vascular, neoplastic, and degenerative conditions and nutritional deficiency. Diseases that also occur in younger patients may be modified by increasing age, or obscured by other conditions. In addition, diseases for which treatment may be indicated in younger persons, such as mild diabetes or hypertension or even cancer, may be better left untreated in the elderly, since for them the treatment may be worse than the disease and the long-term sequelae of the disease will not be effected by treatment.

Disability: This must be recognized as a factor in geriatric illness that merits assessment and treatment distinct from the disease processes that may underlie it.

Mental capacity: It is essential to assess mental capacity (especially understanding, initiative, and willingness) as a factor affecting the prospects of elderly patients.

Social background: The complex part played by environmental and other social factors is often of overriding importance in long-term care. After retirement, people enter a phase of life when social factors become increasingly important; in addition, relatives and friends are also older and less able to help if illness develops.

The interdisciplinary approach is a cornerstone of long-term care. Long-term care calls for much more of this approach than the physician usually is comfortable with. If it is to succeed, more than lip service is required. This approach demands of the various health disciplines a coordination that may be difficult to achieve, in which the elderly patient, the family, and various professions take a part. Coordination and cooperation are most effective if each participant clearly respects the limit of his own experience and legitimate interests, and thus respects the insight and integrity of the others. Using the interdisciplinary approach, it becomes obvious that there is significant overlap of professional turf among medical personnel. Some specific areas that should be watched for are overlaps between: occupational therapy and physical therapy, recreational therapy and occupational therapy, social work and nursing, occupational therapy and social work, physician and nurse.

It becomes clear that at least a working knowledge by the physician of the professional turf of the other important health professionals involved in long-term care is essential if this interdisciplinary approach is to succeed. In preparing physicians to assume a more active role in long-term care, these special issues should be emphasized in medical training. Typically, practicing physicians have not benefited from such training and may not consider these issues in treating elderly patients in all settings.

The Physician's Role in Day Care

Day care is an example of a long-term care model and it represents a particular challenge for the physician. The physician's role is summarized in Table 6.1.

Table 6.1   Physician Responsibilities in Day Care

Direct Role	Indirect Role[b]

1. patient care
    at the center[a]
    in the community
2. treatment plan
3. referrals
	1. utilization review
	2. program evaluation
	3. treatment plan development
	4. standing orders

[a] Usually available only from staff physician.
[b] Minimal involvement from community physician.

Direct and indirect physician involvement may be provided by physicians under contract with the day care center, by physicians on the staff of the center or the institution in which the center is based, or by community-based physicians. The indirect role, although very important, is also more difficult to maintain unless the physician is on the staff of the day care center.

The direct care responsibilities of physicians fall into two major areas: on-site care and community-based care. The on-site care may involve screening histories and physicals of newly admitted patients; evaluating accidents that occur at the centers, which are not infrequent given the activity and fragility of the patients; evaluating acute episodes of illness (e.g., flu, diarrhea, chest pain); and reevaluating treatment regimens.

Community-based care is the care rendered in the physician's private office in the community or in the community hospital. In these cases the patient is usually transported to the physician's office and all arrangements are made by the day care center staff. Community-based care reflects minimal physician involvement with the formal day care program. This form of medical service delivery now dominates in most centers in the United States. The goal of the future should be to increase both forms of physician involvement and thereby increase the potential of day care centers to deliver ambulatory health care to the aged.

It seems evident that the on-site patient care and the community-based care may present problems, since different physicians are usually involved. At times it is difficult for the community-based physician to coordinate efforts with the medical staff of the center. The center staff may find it problematic to change the patient's treatment and medication as the need arises because the community physician either is not readily accessible or refuses to change the treatment regimen. Cases arise, for example, in which the center physician recommends a change in the amount of the patient's tranquilizers or bedtime sedation as the patient's condition changes and the community physician disagrees and recommends a nursing-home placement instead. Despite the presence of medical staff at the center, a community physician remains in charge of the patient and thus may be called to see him at night or during weekends.

A patient may have several community physicians because of "physician shopping" or because several specialists are needed to handle his diverse medical needs. Day care center staff often report that it is impossible to sustain a treatment regimen prescribed by many physicians. This problem is especially critical in the area of drug prescriptions. It is common for some patients to be at one time on eight or more drugs prescribed by different physicians. Clearly, this situation is complicated, but a system developed in England has potential application in America: Two treatment cards are made out for each patient. One is left in his center record, the other is sent home with the patient in an envelope to be brought back each day he attends the center. Any changes made by the community practitioner or center staff are noted on this card and so each is aware of the drugs being given.

Another system that has been found to be useful is the use of a Dosett.® This is a plastic device that enables the staff to make up one week's medicine for daily drug intake by the patient and has been found to be particularly useful for day care patients on multiple drug regimens.[2]

Another approach to the drug problem is to develop stop orders similar to such orders in hospitals for certain drugs. For day care the particular areas of concern are for such drugs as tranquilizers, sedatives, vitamins, arthritis medicine, antivertigo medicine, iron tablets, pain medicine, anticonvulsants, diuretics, oral hypoglycemic agents, and antibiotics. The urge to prescribe is great and oftentimes the medications are continued long after they cease to be appropriate. Not infrequently the patient does better when all the medications are stopped. The day care center may have more rehabilitation potential than the referring physician realizes.

A close cooperative relationship between the community physician and the day center staff is essential to handle drug-related problems, rehabilitation services, and many other problems. A successful approach to solve the problems includes: allowing the patient to continue to receive services from his referring physician or community physician, insuring that there is a physician accessible to the patient during those periods when the patient is not present at the day care center, helping to avoid unnecessary expenditure of the physician's time by handling certain problems with standing orders, having the community physician recognize the ongoing knowledge that the center staff has of the patient and allow for changes in the patient's treatment regimen accordingly. For example:

A 64-year-old female school teacher was referred to the Lexington center by her husband because she was depressed. She had been in an automobile accident and sustained a brain injury resulting in a right hemiparesis and memory loss. She was discharged from the hospital after rehabilitation, but failed to improve at home and became more disabled and depressed. Although she was led to believe she had little rehabilitation potential, she received physical, recreational, and occupational therapy at the center, socialized well, and was able to recover sufficiently to return to teaching.

The relationship of the community physician to the center nursing and physician staff should be similar to that between a physician and the specialist to whom he refers a patient or to that between the community physician and the nurses and resident physicians on hospital wards. Even more than in hospitals, the center staff has prolonged and continual contact with the patient. The patient's condition, while usually not acute, is fragile and constantly fluctuating and requires changes in treatment modalities and drugs. Thus, the nurse and other professional members of the center may request therapy changes that need to be approved by the staff physician and should then be coordinated with the community physician. As does a specialist to whom a physician refers a patient, the center staff should have the flexibility to modify the treatment regimen in cooperation with the community physician or referring physician, who retains the primary responsibility for the patient.

Another direct role of the physician is in development of treatment plans for the patient. All too often this is done without any real interchange with the other health professionals involved in the patient's care. The plan should be an interdisciplinary product that assesses the patient's diagnoses, disabilities, mental capacity, and social functioning. Some appropriate patient assessment instrument should be chosen from the many that are available (see chapters 4, 5, and 11). Specifically, the Lexington center utilizes the battery developed by Katz et al.,[3] and objectives for the patient are worked out (three-month goals and long-term goals) involving at a minimum the patient, his family, a nurse, a social worker, and the physician. These goals are necessary to provide the proper enriching therapeutic milieu at the center and to help families develop realistic expectations for the patient.

The center staff also needs the treatment goals to direct their activities, determine outcome, and enhance the reality of their expectations. Without the goals, which are the major criteria for judging the success of care, the staff will feel frustrated and futile (as is not uncommon in nursing homes).

Specialized Activities

Referrals are another direct responsibility of the physician. Differing from most other health care facilities, however, a day care center need not require the participant to be admitted by a physician. Although the usual pattern is for the patient to have a community-based private physician, a patient may be referred by himself or by his family, a friend, or a community agency. This means that the physician may be reacting to a situation rather than instigating an action. To avoid providing the physician with ex post facto knowledge about referrals not initiated by him, some day care centers, such as Levindale, have developed formats for notification of the physician at the time of application.

Proper referral by a community physician to a day care center is essential, however, because of the involvement that it requires and for the patient's benefit. Furthermore, the physician's attitude is often crucial to whether or not the patient attends the day center. Where the family has any doubt about its ability, or willingness, to care for the patient at home, the most meaningful and effective reassurance they can get is from the physician himself. In addition, patients frequently have misgivings about going to the day care center either because they feel "too sick" or are just anxious about the new adventure. The physician's reassurance is most effective here, too.

When the patient is referred by someone other than a physician, it may be very difficult to have any physician assume direct role responsibilities. An attitude not infrequently expressed in such cases is "the patient can go to the center but it won't help," or "he is a hopeless case so it doesn't matter what you do," or "the outing may be of some benefit." An example of such a case can illustrate this point:

> A 71-year-old lady was referred to the center by her neighbors. She had diabetes mellitus, hypertension, and gout, and was confined to a wheelchair, withdrawn, and totally dependent on her neighbors for medications, meals, and personal care. She was not given much rehabilitation potential by the physician, who frequently changed her treatments. At the center her medications were regulated and monitored, she received physical and occupational therapy, and recreational therapy.

After attending two years, she was able to walk with a cane, do her own housework and grocery shopping, and was socializing well. At that time her discharged was planned.

In general, admission should be considered not as a last resort but as an appropriate treatment for the elderly infirm who need more therapeutic support than can be provided in the home but do not require hospitalization or nursing-home care. Sometimes this support must be provided over a long period before any results are seen. It is important also to emphasize day care as a therapeutic model whose benefits are greater than the mere sum of its individual components. The center is not just a diversional activity to entertain socially the lonely elderly or just a nursing home without the hotel services.

In addition, when a physician refers a patient to the center it is helpful to think in terms of all the long-term care components. Functional capabilities should be emphasized rather than disease categories. The functional areas for which services are prescribed most often for day care patients are:

1. to improve ambulation, transfer, mobility, and physical activities, and to increase their safety,

2. to improve participation and endurance in activities of daily living,

3. to improve range of motion of affected extremities,

4. to improve mental status (to improve reality orientation and attention span, to decrease depression, and to increase social participation).

Over 80 percent of the patients enrolled at both centers in Lexington have the following primary diagnosis: diabetes, hypertension, stroke and residuals, arteriosclerotic cardiovascular disease, congestive heart failure, arthritis, and neurosensory problems. However, a medical diagnosis may have little to do with the reasons for the patient's admission. Frequently, the main medical condition affecting the patient is less disabling than some apparently trivial one. For example, the patient may suffer from severe arthritis, yet his main handicap may be poor vision. With glasses he may readily adjust to his more serious condition and make adequate compensations.

An example of a typical appropriate referral to a day center program may be beneficial:

> An 84-year-old gentleman had been hospitalized three times in one year. Each time his hospitalization resulted from inadequate care of his diabetes mellitus. The patient was an unusual diabetic in that he was extremely brittle and very sensitive to insulin. A major problem when he went home was that he became very depressed and did not eat, and then began bouncing into insulin overkill phenomena. He had a most depressive home atmosphere. His 88-year-old wife was very self-centered, dominant, and reclusive. During his hospitalization she did not visit him. She was also ill, but was not as incapacitated as her husband. He was admitted to a nursing home for nearly a month in an attempt to alleviate the situation, and he did beautifully there for a while, but unfortunately he signed himself out against medical advice because he wanted to be in his own home. The patient was quite mentally alert and capable and was totally agreeable to going to the day care center five days a week. The patient has done excellently at the Lexington center, where the wife has also gotten involved.

One of the most important indirect roles for the physician in day care is utilization review and intake procedures. The process combines the functions of a case conference, hospital ward rounds, and peer review. It is another component of day care in which the interdisciplinary approach is so vital. Each patient should be reviewed at least every three months and when significant changes occur. This review should cover the following points:

1. Is admission appropriate? What are the medical, social, and rehabilitative problems?

2. What other services would be appropriate (e.g., home health care, homemaker service, nutrition centers, foster homes)?

3. Is the frequency of attendance appropriate? How many days a week should the patient attend? What alternatives to attending are available?

4. Are the treatment modalities appropriate in type and frequency? What services are needed: recreational, physical, occupational, speech therapies; social work; nutrition; physical attention; medicines?

5. What other community resources should be used?

6. When can the patient be discharged or when can his attendance be reduced?

In reviewing each patient, specific competencies must be examined.[4] The following areas are included:

1. physiologic and medical functioning of vital systems and organs, medications (information provided by the physician and nurse),

2. physical functioning of major antigravity muscles and support structures, use of upper limbs (information provided by the occupational, physical, and recreational therapists),

3. domestic activities of daily living, speech (information provided by nutritionist, speech therapist, and occupational therapist),

4. emotional, social, and intellectual functioning (information provided by the social worker and recreational therapist),

5. economic functioning, financial status (information provided by the social worker).

Any defects in these areas must be addressed when the patient is admitted to the center and during utilization review. The service and treatment plan must be carefully formulated so that it meets the patient's need without producing overdependence on the center.

Dependence on the center can present serious problems for the physician and staff at the time of utilization review and discharge. The patient may be functionally ready for discharge, but because of his dependence on the center, the discharge could result in a setback in the patient's condition. The staff also can become dependent on the patient because of his or her improvement and cooperation. This is a problem in long-term care and needs to be addressed and dealt with. Day care centers create an appetite among old people for companionship and purposeful activity. It has been suggested that this is a form of emotional dependence; perhaps it is unfortunate, but physicians must accept it. The importance to positive health of companionship and purpose in old age must be recognized. It is one of the therapeutic modalities at day care centers. To deal with the problem the community must provide for these needs by establishing social day care centers and other community support activities, such as nutrition centers and Retired Senior Volunteer Programs. On Lok is the only day care center that has provided such a service for its participants by developing a social center unit (see chapter 3). Many patients have also become volunteers at centers and enjoy the continuing relationship as a transition back to more independent living.

Participants should be told on admission that as they improve and no longer need the center their spot will have to go to one of the many needy persons on the waiting list. If this is done early on in the course of the person's stay, the problems are lessened.

Another important function of the intake procedure is to provide for a proper patient mix at the centers. The patient census should not be overloaded with serious cases (e.g., severely disoriented or preterminal cases). An overload of serious cases can detract from the therapeutic milieu and frustrate the staff. Mixing participants, although accepted in Europe, is not practiced in this country. In fact, there is a tendency to classify nursing homes and day care centers so that a proper patient mix is impossible. Staff and patients need the successes of less demanding cases to sustain morale and act as a model for other patients.

The physician also has an important role to play in sustaining good staff morale at the center by providing the ongoing medical backup, consultation, and inservice training that is needed. It has been found that to have no readily available physician is very demoralizing to center staff. Furthermore, he or she must help create an atmosphere in which the activity is directed toward stimulating the participants and the center staff.[5] The physician needs to encourage this or it will not be sustained or may be misguided.

Other important indirect roles for the physician are program evaluation, treatment plan development (in case conferences), and the development of standing orders. Program evaluation should include examination of the quality of care by chart review and by assisting in the development and application of assessment instruments to determine overall program success in meeting their objectives (see chapter 11).

The various health professionals delivering services at the center need standing orders for the procedures for treatment of such conditions as diarrhea, constipation, and upper respiratory infections; when to order laboratory tests; when ultrasound is indicated; when the aides are to assist in physical, occupational, and speech therapy; changes in medication; stop orders for medications. When standing orders are not available, there is a tendency for the center staff to assume either more or less responsibility than is appropriate for quality patient care.

Conclusion

The physician has a pivotal role to play in the delivery of services in the adult day care setting. However, this role is not the traditional one, and requires new responsibilities, a change in the relationship with the patient, and substantial interaction with professional staff at the day care centers.

Notes

1. Charles H. Percy, "Medicine and Aging: An Assessment of Opportunities and Neglect," opening statement for a hearing, U.S. Senate Special Committee on Aging, New York City, October 13, 1976.

2. Dosett, U. S. Patent Nos. 3537422, 3618, 557, Eh Farma, S-102 25, Stockholm 12, Sweden; C. Herdenstam, "Greater Reliability in the Handling of Drugs in Non-Institutional Medical Care," Nynoshami Hospital, *Lakartidningen,* vol. 70, 1973, pp. 2247–2248; Mats Pers, "Experiments in Long-Term Treatment in an Outpatient Department," *Lakartidningen,* vol. 66, 1969, pp. 750–751.

3. Sidney Katz et al., *Effects of Continued Care: A Study of Chronic Illness in the Home* (Washington, D.C.: National Center for Health Services Research and Development, Health Services and Mental Health Administration, Department of Health, Education and Welfare, December, 1972); Sidney Katz et al., "Progress in Development of the Index of ADL," *The Gerontologist,* part I, Spring 1970, pp. 20–30; Sidney Katz et al., "Studies of Illness in the Aged; The Index of ADL: A Standardized Measure of Biological and Psychosocial Function," *Journal of the American Medical Association,* vol. 185, 1963, pp. 914–919.

4. L. Z. Cosin, "Rehabilitation of the Older Patient," *World Hospitals,* vol. 9, edition 4, October 1973.

5. Lars Linder, "Factors to Consider in Long-Term Care," unpublished paper, Kungsgardets Hospital, Uppsala, Sweden, September 1974.

Useful Readings

Education and Training in Long-Term and Geriatric Care, report on a Working Group convened by the World Health Organization Regional Office for Europe (Copenhagen, Denmark: World Health Organization, 1973).

Forrest, G. Gressler, *Patient Care Assessment in Extended Health Care Facilities* (New Haven, Conn.: Connecticut Health Services Research Series, no. 6, 1975).

Morton, E. B., "Advances in Geriatrics," *The Practitioner,* vol. 203, October 1969, pp. 525–533.

Sawson, I. R., and Ingman, Stanley, eds., *The Language of Geriatric Care: Implications for Professional Review* (New Haven, Conn.: Connecticut Health Services Research Series, no. 6, 1975).

Winds of Change, a report of a Conference on Activity Programs in Long-Term Care Institutions (Chicago, Ill.: American Hospital Association, 1971).

Working with Older People: A Guide to Practice, volumes 1–4, (Rockville, Md.: Health Services and Mental Health Administration, Department of Health, Education and Welfare, May 1972).

7

Restoring and Maintaining Functional Capacities

Introduction

Nutritionists, occupational therapists, physical therapists, and recreational therapists are essential to an adult day care program. However, unlike a number of other supporting professionals (such as dentists, podiatrists, speech therapists, ophthalmologists, and otolaryngologists), they must modify their methods to fit the specialized environment of day care.

Rehabilitation has been defined as ". . . restoration of the handicapped to the fullest physical, mental, social, vocational, and economic usefulness of which they are capable."[1] This definition applies to elderly persons as well as to the younger handicapped. Restoring and maintaining elderly persons at their maximal functional capacity must be an interdisciplinary effort. Although not all members of the team must be simultaneously involved with a patient, it is crucial that each member have some input into patient assessment, care planning, implementation of the plan, and evaluation of outcomes.

Nutrition Needs and Services

Nutritional services play a pivotal role in adult day care. Maintaining an adequate nutritional intake is very important for the aging person, particularly for one who is physically or mentally ill. Malnutrition may be responsible for many complaints of general weakness, or irritability and other psychological symptoms. The deficiencies lie primarily in inadequate intake of protein, calcium, and essential vitamins. As a rule, older people have a reduced water intake and characteristically develop a preference for sugars. Many tend to eat easily prepared foods that lack nutritional value.

Lacking motivation for adequate meal planning and preparation, the aged person may fall into a vicious cycle of poor nutritional intake leading to lowered energy leading to further poor nutritional intake. Limited income may make it impossible to buy adequate amounts and the right kinds of food. Unfortunately, when income is reduced, one of the first areas of the budget to be cut is that allotted for food, particularly meat, because it is felt that rent and utilities must be paid in order to survive. Inadequate income may cause the older person to buy food in small quantities, which, in the long run, costs more. Meager cooking facilities and refrigeration, which may also result from inadequate income, also contribute to malnutrition.

Inadequate dentition creates difficulties in eating. The partially or completely edentulous person may be unable to chew meats or fresh vegetables and fruits, and thus may restrict his diet to soft, starchy foods. Fewer active taste buds, diminished acuity of sight and smell, and lessened motor skills can contribute to a deficient intake of food. Absorption may be impaired because of a reduction in the quantity of digestive enzymes and gastric acidity. Loneliness, unhappiness, anxiety, or living alone may affect the incentive to eat. The appetite may also be decreased by reduced activity and increased fatigue or weakness. Obesity and inadequate protein intake may also be associated with aging. As people get older, they usually decrease their activity level, but not always their food intake. With the aging process comes a gradual reduction in the basal metabolic rate and a corresponding decrease in caloric need. On the other hand, protein intake is of considerable importance in relation to activity. The above-mentioned deterioration of eating habits may be further complicated by inactivity, resulting in actual loss of protein.

The nutrition component of the treatment plan provides the individual with a balanced and adequate intake of the basic food groups to reach and keep a better health state. How much a person should eat depends on his or her energy needs and specific physiologic requirements. It is imperative, therefore, that advice on nutrition and calories be individualized and based on activity and exercise needs. The nutritionist should work closely with the physical educationist and the recreational and physical therapist to develop exercise programs for the elderly to incorporate into their life style and nutritional intake.

When making recommendations for an adequate, balanced food intake, every attempt should be made to include and retain as much as possible the person's present food customs. It is likely that the recommended changes for an improved diet will not be adhered to over a prolonged period unless consideration is given to socioeconomic, educational, religious, and cultural factors. To assist in this planning, it is a good idea to get a diet history: either a three-day record, which is preferable, or a 24-hour recall of foods eaten. The diet history should also include such information as who prepares the meals and does the food purchasing.

Because digestive processes slow down with age, it may be appropriate to adjust meal size and frequency. Small, frequent meals may be more easily assimilated than the customary two or three large meals a day. In a day care setting, this may be accomplished by mid-morning and mid-afternoon snacks as well as lunch. These snacks should be nutritious and appetizing, and participants should be encouraged to work with staff in selecting appropriate foods.

Because a person is elderly does not mean that he will not be able to learn new ways of eating. Where learning ability is decreased, it is more likely to be the result of some prior incapacity or debilitating health change in the individual. Special efforts must be made to teach new and better ways of eating. The adult day care center provides exciting opportunities for nutrition education.

To provide realistic therapeutic activities for participants requiring assistance with cooking or food serving skills, actual supervised and guided practice may be given as the participant assists, as appropriate, with food preparation and serving at the center. Cafeteria-style serving can be an invaluable method of teaching appropriate food selection. Supervised group or individual shopping can demonstrate healthful and economical purchase of food. The use of group teaching allows sharing of ideas and problems among participants.

The staff nutritionist at the Lexington center and the nutrition consultant at the Levindale center have been important in helping staff investigate the cases of patients refusing to eat and helping determine how these cases could be better managed.

> A 74-year-old man was admitted to the Lexington center with severe muscular disabilities due to repeated strokes, complicated by diabetes and a need for a special diet. The combination of problems caused the man to be unable to swallow properly and he experienced spilling and choking while eating. The nutritionist worked with the speech and occupational therapists to develop the proper nutritional program. The speech therapists helped to communicate the man's dietary history and the occupational therapist helped to develop his skills to improve chewing and swallowing. Thus, the nutritionist developed a program that met nutritional requirements, dietary preferences, and functional capabilities. This helped him to improve socialization during the meal period.

The values of the social component of eating cannot be overestimated. Eating is a social behavior that has been greatly emphasized in our culture. Take, as examples of the rituals associated with eating, the rules of etiquette designed to make the process more esthetic to fellow diners, or customs related to preparation and serving. Eating is much more pleasurable when shared with someone. The social aspects of eating are lacking for many elderly who live and eat alone. Therefore, an important benefit to adult day care participants is the socialization during meals. This can be enhanced by the use of small tables, seating six or fewer, rather than long banquet-style tables. Special effort should be given to creating an atmosphere conducive to good food intake, using lighting, topics of conversation, permanent dinner and silverware rather than disposable plates and utensils, attractive serving procedures, tablecloths, and centerpieces.

The use of music in establishing an atmosphere conducive to eating is widely accepted. Music selected to meet the general desires of the group can be an asset in promoting adequate eating and digestion.

The activities of eating, serving, and meal preparation can be useful mechanisms for implementing occupational and recreational therapy programs. For example, the occupational therapist may recommend adaptations to enhance independence in eating or may develop with the nutritionist a program of supervised practice leading toward greater independence in meal preparation.

Recreational Needs and Services

Our society is oriented toward work and productive activity. Older individuals often are unprepared to cope with leisure time. For many, retirement symbolizes the uselessness to which society has relegated the aged.

Over the past few years, various kinds of social centers for elderly persons have been developed, but older people with disabilities do not fit in or are not welcome in these socially oriented groups. There is a need, then, for constructive leisure activities or recreation for impaired individuals.

Recreation means restoration or renewal. Kaplan has suggested the following objectives of recreation: companionship and fun, a sense of belonging to the community, a feeling of contentment, an opportunity to receive recognition, an outlet to develop new interests and skills and retain or renew old ones, an occasion for both continuous learning experience and arousing interest in order to stimulate learning, assistance to adjust in a changing environment, assistance with dispelling the attitude of "what's the use, since I'm now too old," offsetting the deadening effects of loneliness and aloneness, parrying the consequences of reduced income, and replacing declining health with more efficient use of remaining capacities.[2]

The recreation therapist is one of the newest members of the day care staff, and fills the need for expert avocational guidance, particularly for elderly persons who are isolated and less socially oriented. An individualized recreation plan can provide real motivation and impetus to a participant to return to the center to receive other therapies that may not be as pleasant but are equally as important. Active participation in stimulating, enjoyable activities can be the focal point of a patient's day. It is crucial, therefore, that participants have choices and input in planning their individualized activities programs.

The mood and atmosphere of the center can be greatly influenced by recreational activities. There is a fine line between activities considered adult-oriented and those considered child-oriented. Emphasis should be placed on individual and group activities that are therapeutic, meaningful, stimulating, and appropriate to the individual's abilities and interests. The approach to the participant is very important. If each activity has a therapeutic purpose and is presented to the participant in a mature manner, it will more likely be accepted as such. The level of sophistication and involvement depends on the participant's abilities. For example, beads can be used with individuals of varying abilities and may range from simple stringing to complex jewelry designing.

Activities may range from very spontaneous to very structured, and it is important to maintain a balance between these two extremes. Activities are not necessarily better because they are planned and structured. Creative and enhancing recreation combines both options and provides an opportunity for individual choice.

Who should decide how much a participant should utilize recreational therapy? It is important that participants be allowed to function at a pace comfortable for them, because too much pressure for involvement can be destructive for the resistive participant. However, every participant should be involved in some activity and the recreational therapist must decide, on an individual basis, how much to encourage. If nonparticipation is a frequently occurring problem, it may be necessary to involve the other team members in reassessment and replanning.

Participants are more apt to become involved in activities when they perceive the activities as useful, for example, making toys for a children's party. The making and sale of arts and crafts items by center participants is also a means of enhancing self-worth, for it shows society that older persons are still productive. The money from these items can be given to the participants or used to purchase more arts and crafts supplies.

The skills of the recreational therapist are also important for recruiting, training, and supervising volunteers. Effective use of volunteers can expand staff capabilities while maintaining quality. Successful rehabilitation of participants can result in an additional reservoir of volunteers who have intimate experiences with the system and can provide insightful assistance.

There are some areas of recreation that the recreational therapist may tend to avoid because the activity is not considered appropriate for older persons. However, many active games and sports can be adapted for use with elderly or impaired individuals and will be very stimulating and enjoyable. For example, even a person in a wheelchair can participate in zoned volleyball. An easily accessible therapeutic tool that can be used to great advantage is the outdoors. Walks, croquet, wheelchair gardens, and garden clubs are enjoyable and therapeutic activities.

Music in the recreational program is valuable. There are several avenues for participation: singing, playing instruments, critical listening, and dancing. Dancing is simply motion to music; geriatric participation may range from swaying and fingersnapping to more traditional group dances. The recreational therapist can develop some basic techniques of music and dance therapy through consultation with therapists who specialize in these art forms.

Religion plays an important part in the lives of elderly persons. Almost all older people admit to belief in God and verbally acknowledge the importance of religion. A person's concept of death is related to his view of religion. Prayer, hymn singing, and reading religious books can be integral components of the activities program and may be intiated by the participants themselves.

Special events, such as holidays, birthdays, field trips, and outside speakers, can be important occasions for adult day care participants and can provide an exciting change from everyday routines.

Because elderly persons frequently have decreased social interactions, improved socialization or social interaction must be a goal of recreational therapy. McCuan and Levenson report increased verbal and physical interaction as results of planned small group activities and crafts projects in a day care setting, and find that grouping participants with mixed levels of physical and mental impairment creates greater group stimulation. They conclude that programs designed to encourage maximum social functioning of each individual must be conducted by a skilled, sensitive person who is able to establish a one-to-one relationship with an individual and then use the relationship as a bridge to establish communication and interaction among the participants in the group.[3]

The recreational therapist must be creative and flexible, and should be able to improvise to provide a high-quality activities program on a sometimes limited budget. The most essential guideline, however, is to involve the participant in developing a plan which meets his or her own interests, capabilities, and therapeutic needs.

Occupational Therapy Needs and Services

The occupational therapist is a long-standing member of the rehabilitation team whose techniques are designed to increase range of motion, strength, dexterity, and coordination. Through craft techniques, the occupational therapist can control sensory-motor behavior and improve basic neurophysiological functioning. Responsibility for securing, either by purchase or innovation, the variety of adaptive devices the patient needs to accomplish certain activities of daily living rests with the occupational therapist. He or she can also assess a patient's home environment and recommend modifications and adaptations for safety, independence, and convenience.

A unique feature of occupational therapy in a geriatric day care setting is the increased responsibility for development of the plan of therapy. The therapist evaluates the patient, develops an appropriate plan, and confers with the physician to obtain medical authorization. This often is not the case in a hospital or extended care facility, where the physician generates the plan and the therapist implements it. In adult day care, the methods of implementation of an occupational therapy plan are directly related to and determined by the imagination, creativity, and ingenuity of the therapist, and may range from simple adaptations to the sophisticated level of a sheltered workshop. Many media may be used for meeting the goals of proper positioning and coordination, gross movement, range of motion, strengthening, appropriate use of devices, perceptual motor functioning, and activities of daily living.

In the adult day care setting, the occupational therapist may depend more heavily on paraprofessionals or aides to implement the plan of therapy and thus be able to expand capabilities. Working with groups of persons with similar physical disabilities is a very effective therapeutic method that can be used for the encouragement and support of individual members.

Physical Therapy Needs and Services

The primary responsibility of the physical therapist is to provide treatment using such methods as exercise, heat, cold, whirlpool, ultrasound, and diathermy in the areas of ambulation, gait training, transferring techniques, assistance with prosthetic devices, maintenance of joint motion, and prevention of disability from degenerative joint diseases.

The physical therapist has a unique role and increased responsibility for development of the plan of therapy in a geriatric day care setting. Most often the patient is seen first by the physical therapist, who evaluates the patient and develops an appropriate plan and then requests physician input and authorization. This is not usually the case in an impatient setting, where the physician initiates the plan of care.

Creativity, flexibility, and improvisational skills are important assets for a physical therapist. More often than not, there may be limited physical equipment and space so that the imagination is taxed to supply appropriate aids. There may be a mix of patients with different types and levels of disability.

The use of groups having similar physical disabilities or therapeutic needs is effective. The physical therapist is equipped by education and experience to undertake the task of providing safe, effective exercise programs for elderly patients; this is a critical prevention effort that should be a part of the day care program. The therapist is in a critical position to detect early signs and symptoms of disability that may be improved or contained by early initiation of an appropriate plan. There is an opportunity to emphasize the preventive treatment of progressive diseases not possible in an inpatient setting, where physical therapy usually stops at the end of acute care.

There is an important teaching role for the therapist in day centers. Implementation of the treatment plan requires the involvement of others—paraprofessionals or aides, the participant, and the family—because, to be effective, physical therapy must be carried out daily. The fact that physical therapy must be done on those days when the participant is not at the center puts greater responsibility on the participant and the family for follow-through.

Conclusion

Providing rehabilitative or maintenance services in a geriatric day setting has exciting ramifications. Physical therapy and occupational therapy can set the whole tone for a day care program; this is the case in many British centers. Nutritional services and counseling can also play a lead role and act as the core of activities at a day center. There is tremendous potential for cooperation in the joint implementation and delivery of various health services. For example, a participant with decreased manual dexterity may have an occupational therapy goal of buttoning his shirt with a plan developed for increasing manual dexterity. This can also be supported in the recreational therapy program by encouraging participation in activities requiring fine motor skills of the hand and fingers, such as Chinese checkers. The physical therapist and nutritionist may collaborate and jointly implement a program related to diet and exercise. Such an exercise program has been successfully developed at the Lexington day care center. These examples emphasize how one therapeutic activity can and should complement another.

There is the possibility of the extension of services beyond the center. Staff members can, as necessary, modify and adapt the home environment, work intensively with family or significant others, and actually implement the plan of treatment in the home. For example, assisting an elderly housewife to assume modified meal preparation responsibilities may involve an evaluation and modification of her kitchen. The maintenance or restoration of function in elderly persons in a day care setting is a challenging and satisfying activity for health professionals and has as its reward the maintenance of an individual outside an institution.

Notes

1. Commission on Chronic Illness, *Chronic Illness in the United States: Care of the Long-Term Patient* (Cambridge, Mass.: Harvard University Press, 1956), p. 170; R. E. Irvine, M.D., "Physiotherapy and the Geriatric Day Hospital," *Physiotherapy*, no. 55, 1969, pp. 352–357.

2. Jerome Kaplan, "Satisfying Use of Time," in *Working with Older People: A Guide to Practice, Volume III: The Aging Person: Needs and Services* (Washington, D.C.: U.S. Government Printing Office, Department of Health, Education, and Welfare, publication no. HSM 72–6007, 1972), p. 47.

3. Eloise Rathbone-McCuan and Julia Levenson, "Impact of Socialization Therapy in a Geriatric Day Care Setting," *Gerontologist,* vol. 15, 1975, pp. 338–342.

8

The Role
of the Social Worker

Introduction

In the past few years, social workers have begun to assume a primary role in the delivery of health, social, and mental health services to the aged, and it can be anticipated that their activities will increase and become more diversified. As Brody and Brody have said:

> ... a critical role of social work with respect to the aged for the decade of the eighties is fulfilling the primary responsibility of advocacy. Advocacy in turn must be supported by research, education, and service. Certainly, the broad goals are to reduce socially induced risks: negative attitudes, poverty, vulnerability due to minority group status, environmental stresses such as poor housing and dangerous neighborhoods, and neglect in health services.[1]

From the initial intake through the treatment program to discharge, the social worker must play an active part in the total care of participants in day care centers. The responsibilities assumed by social work personnel in day care centers range from administrative to direct clinical services. A variety of practice methods can be employed, and nonprofessional staff and volunteers can be used as an effective complement to professional and paraprofessional social workers.

Administrative/Managerial Responsibilities

In most geriatric day care programs, social workers have some type of administrative responsibility. There are two general patterns: total responsibility and partial responsibility. In the total leadership pattern, the professional social worker is the administrative head of the entire program with broad administrative authority sanctioned by the program's organizational structure. In the partial leadership pattern, the professional social worker is the supervisor of all social services.

Resource allocation is one administrative responsibility that highlights the difference between the total and partial patterns. The total administrator differentiates the essential services of the program from those that only supplement the basic services, and controls all fiscal decision-making, sets priorities for each service component, and makes the most beneficial resource allocations. The partial administrator is an advocate for personal service priorities, and documents the need for social services and how such services benefit the participants. This documentation must clearly spell out the reasons for continued or expanded social work services.

The administrative pattern influences the program's service orientation: When a social worker assumes total leadership, greater emphasis usually is placed on the social functioning of participants, programming tends to focus on activities and therapies to facilitate resocialization, and the various health functions structured into the social services are of secondary importance. The Levindale center is so structured and places service emphasis on the delivery of social-health services to the impaired elderly. The Lexington center, which uses a nurse as the administrative head, developed a unique pattern of administrative leadership under shared authority between a nurse and a social worker. In this program the social worker supervises all social service personnel at the day care center. Social services are only one in an array of various rehabilitative services offered.

Utilizing either administrative pattern, the social worker should be engaged in program planning and policy development. These are key components in any well-organized day care program, and are critical when the service has a long-term orientation. Program planning includes integrating social work services with health services. Policy development involves setting priorities and areas of emphasis.

In the program planning process, the social worker helps create plans to meet the psychosocial needs of participants. First, the social worker determines the primary needs of all participants (by a thorough review of assessments and participant care plans). Secondly, appropriate interventive strategies are selected for delivering services, and methods for implementation of these strategies are delineated. Finally, quantitative measures are formulated for evaluating the services provided. The social worker is involved in this process along with all staff at the day care center, working closely with the director and others charged with administrative responsibility to ensure that the center's objectives, methods, and evaluation reflect the social work efforts.

The social worker's supervisory functions are also important. For example, at Lexington, social work personnel were added to the center gradually because the sponsoring organization (the health department) had not developed a social work unit. The first professional worker to be hired was a health department staff person who assumed simultaneous responsibility for supervising the day care center through a consultation relationship with the day care health professionals. Subsequently, a social worker with a baccalaureate degree was hired, and the professional social worker then devoted more time to supervising this worker, who in turn was part of the interdisciplinary team. Eventually, additional social service components were added to strengthen the service. Current patterns of supervision tend to emphasize maximum supervision by the professional social worker of the health department staff.

The pattern of supervision at Levindale also evolved over time. During the early stages of the program, the part-time professional social worker was not receiving formal clinical supervision, but was supervising other day care staff through the interdisciplinary-team approach. During the second year of the center's operation, the Levindale inpatient department of social work was expanded and included a director of social services who, as administrative head, could provide clinical supervision to all day care staff. The director of social services also provided specialized clinical supervision to the professional day care social worker to help expand the scope of the clinical services that could be offered to participants and their families.

The particular pattern of social work supervision, therefore, depends on the organization structure, staffing patterns, service goals, types of clients, and personalities of individual staff members. Three important principles have emerged from the Lexington and Levindale programs. Patterns of supervision must:

1. foster sufficient staff autonomy to insure incentive for service involvement and accountability,

2. be appropriate for the interdisciplinary team,

3. be adaptable to the changing and expanding needs of the program.

Direct Service Responsibilities

Initial evaluation is one of the social worker's direct service responsibilities. In both the Lexington and Levindale programs, social workers use a variety of instruments[2] to obtain a broad picture of the clinical and social status of the patient. Since the participant's success in the program will depend on stable and strong social supports, this information is vital to the discussions about admissions to the programs. When an elderly person or a family member applies for day care services, it is crucial for the social worker to assess the family environment and identify significant others who will sustain the participant in the home environment. The interaction between the family and the social worker during this time should lead to continued work with the family throughout the participant's involvement with the center. Whenever possible, home visits should be made by the social worker to evaluate the applicant's need for service as well as the living environment. A great deal can be learned through such visits about applicants' abilities to sustain themselves at home.

A critical factor in the intake evaluation is an assessment of the applicant's willingness to be admitted to the program. For many, it is their first experience with a health care program, and they are reluctant to accept help because of fear, uncertainty, or a lack of acceptance of the condition or need for help. This creates conflict with family members who have sought the help and desire that their relative attend the program. The social worker must work to resolve these problems. All alternatives need to be explored with the client and family to make certain that they have selected the most appropriate care for the client. Referral to another program may have to be the alternative, and social work follow-up by the center can be helpful, if time permits.

Centers should adopt the policy that each case is presented for further review and discussion after the client has spent a two-week to four-week trial period at the center. This additional in-center observation helps insure appropriateness of placement.

Another important direct service is participant orientation. The new participant may feel uncomfortable because of the new daily routine, the new physical environment, unwillingness to socialize with other participants (or unwillingness of cliques to welcome newcomers), the sometimes tasking therapeutic routine, and a feeling of abandonment. Here the social worker, as well as other staff members, must support the person. Once the patient has become oriented, it is possible to guide him or her into active participation in the overall plan of care.

The multifaceted needs of the individual require that many services be provided. The social worker assumes two major responsibilities. First, to insure that the social service plan is being implemented. Second, to insure that the individual's psychosocial adjustment to other aspects of the total care plan are constructive. Occasionally, patients are not able to adjust to some parts of the treatment plan or to the total plan. If it is impossible for the person to adjust, the social worker must explain the reason to the other staff. Solutions must arise from a dialogue among the interdisciplinary team members. If, for example, some physical therapy or nursing treatment is not accepted by the patient yet is essential for the individual's progress, the social worker should use a second strategy and help other staff develop an approach that is less traumatic.

Social workers often do not know how to apply traditional clinical methods to aged clients because they are unfamiliar with older people and because psychoanalysis does not seem appropriate for the problems of old age. "The psychoanalytic framework on which much social work is based considers human development only to maturity —the stage attained in adult life."[3] There is a need to expand the framework that guides the therapeutic relation. McCuan has discussed the limitation of the existing theoretical framework, and has advanced the argument for considering the socialization theory used at Levindale in accomplishing some role restoration and new role development through specially developed recreational programming.[4]

Individual resource counseling is an important social service and has been most helpful for persons who experience family or financial problems. Participants are often unaware of the benefits to which they are entitled. One of the most common tasks has been to help persons apply for Medicaid. This frequently requires much of the social worker's time because aged participants find the procedures very complicated and dehumanizing, and because they resist reimbursement as a form of charity. Staff at Lexington report that they need to spend many hours contacting community agencies, and that they must sometimes accompany participants to see that the benefits or services are received.

Group work is another successful direct clinical service. In both Levindale and Lexington, groups are conducted by the social work staff to give participants an opportunity for socialization, self-expression, and decision making. Families benefit from group sessions in which they can discuss common problems and develop supportive links. Generally, the following types of groups have proven valuable in the day center program:

Remotivation and reality: These groups concentrate primarily on remotivating participants who are extremely disoriented; visual stimuli and concentrated social contact are among the techniques used. Memory loss is treated through exercises that focus on tasks designed to orient participants to person, place, and time. Usually, simple techniques of reinforcement are used to change behavior. These techniques are also incorporated into the total treatment program, so that staff are constantly working on the rehabilitation of the participant.

Discussion: Designed for participants who do not have mental impairments and are capable of conversing with others, these groups are concerned primarily with resocialization and attempt to keep mental acuity at an optimal level.

Therapeutic: These groups usually treat specific problems

affecting a sizable number of participants in the program, for example, those who have sustained cerebrovascular accidents or who have emotional problems that interfere with their routine functioning.

Staff: These informal meetings can serve as a forum for staff complaints and as a method of continuing education. In addition, members can discuss their personal feelings regarding the aged and the frustrations encountered with this type of work, which, because of the chronic, long-term nature of many of the patients' problems, often becomes discouraging and depressing to staff.

Discharge Services

At the time of discharge, the social worker is an important link between the participant and the community. For those who have attended the day center for several months, problems associated with disengagement are complex and require preparatory counseling. Many participants are very reluctant to leave the center because it has become a major part of their lives. They do not readily accept other community programs as suitable alternatives to the day center program. The social worker must spend many hours preparing the family and participant for discharge. It is essential that this process begin at the time of admission so that the social worker can build the emotional and social rapport that will insure a successful discharge. It is sometimes difficult for participants to accept discharge as a sign of improvement; often they interpret it as rejection. Family members must also be reassured that they can manage the elderly person without the center's support.

A good relationship with other community agencies and programs is another requirement for successful discharge planning. Most participants need some type of service or volunteer experience after discharge. The social worker, through community resources, can help the participant adjust to a life without the adult day care center. Before discharge, the social worker can take a participant to a nutrition center, for example, to become accustomed to the new service.

Social workers also help in personal, informal follow-up through telephone calls and other contacts with those discharged. Sometimes the discharged person has the opportunity to return to the center as a volunteer and thus maintain social contact.

Conclusion

In the adult day center, the social worker is an integral part of the treatment team. The social work role is extremely important in the planning, development, and provision of services that address the social as well as the health problems of the elderly participants. The worker must not only deliver direct services to clients, but consult with other staff members and assist in program planning. The social/ health day center model requires that social needs be given primary importance, with health services integrated into the basic social services.

As day centers develop and grow in importance, social workers must increase their knowledge and skills in their practice with the elderly client group. Graduate social work programs have recently started to recognize gerontology as an area of specialization, but there is much more to be accomplished to meet the quantitative and qualitative service demands of the present and future.

Notes

1. Elaine M. Brody and Stanley J. Brody, "Decade of Decision for the Elderly," *Social Work,* vol. 19, no. 5, 1974, pp. 544–554.

2. Sidney Katz, *Patient Status Instrument* (East Lansing, Mich.: College of Human Medicine, Michigan State University, 1974); Edith E. Robins, "Therapeutic Day Care: Progress Report on Experiments to Test the Feasibility for Third-Party Reimbursement," paper presented at the 27th Annual Scientific Meeting of the Gerontological Society, Portland, Ore., October 1974.

3. Allen Pencus, "Toward a Developmental View of Aging for Social Work," *Social Work,* vol. 12, 1967, pp. 33–41.

4. Eloise Rathbone-McCuan and Julia Levenson, "Impact of Socialization Therapy in a Geriatric Setting," *Gerontologist,* vol. 15, no. 4, August 1975, pp. 338–342; Eloise Rathbone-McCuan, *An Evaluation of a Geriatric Day Care Center as a Parallel Service to Institutional Care* (Baltimore, Md.: Levindale Geriatric Research Center, 1973).

9

Family as Client

Introduction

Although the participant is the primary consumer of geriatric day care services, the family is another consumer of almost equal importance. The role of the family in the delivery of children's services is a well-accepted fact; the family's role in the planning and delivery of geriatric services is just beginning to be recognized. In this sense, the family is also a day care client. Family involvement with day care begins at the point at which the decision to seek long-term care for the aging member is made, and continues until the termination of that service.

Professionals may neglect the family, and the consequences of this neglect are serious for both the family and the aged person. Neglect may be the result of the professional's decision not to involve the family in the care plan or because the professional lacks the necessary skills to work with the aged and the family as a social unit. For example, the professional may expect the family to commit resources to the care of the aged person without anticipating the long-range burden that will be created for the family, may improperly label the family as neglectful, may apply criteria appropriate for child care, or may not be able to provide integrational family therapy.

Aging and the Family

Contrary to popular belief, families in America do not abandon their aged. While multigenerational living arrangements are not particularly common, interlocking family network systems provide support across generational lines. As the aged family member gradually loses his capacity for independent functioning, other family members from his own and succeeding generations become involved in providing support.[1] Since the family assumes increasing importance to its declining older members, it is necessary to consider the family to fully understand the aging process and to devise support systems for the elderly.

Illness or aging of one family member has an impact on the other family members. Simos reviews the various ways in which life with an aging parent or grandparent affects the family, and finds physical, psychological, social, financial, and housing problems to be the rule rather than the exception.[2] Wasser points out the importance of the family's role in evaluating applications for institutional placement. "The worker should try to comprehend and aid in the adult child's involvement in what is, essentially, a family situation—realizing that the adult child may at times desire to remain outside the situation even though he is obviously involved in it."[3] Brody and Spark remind us of the importance of the historical perspective in that coping mechanisms used to deal with past crises will be used to deal with the crisis of aging.[4]

The most directly affected family members are usually the spouse and the adult, middle-aged children. If there is an intact husband-wife relationship at the first generation, there is a tendency for the first generation to care for each other. For example, an aged husband develops various degrees of impairment so that during the last years of marriage the wife assumes the role of care giver. The critical question, however, is not whether the wife *wants* to assume this role, but whether and for how long she *can*, since she also is likely to be aged and not fully functional.

It is not easy to understand the dynamics of an aged couple without recognizing important personality factors of each member. Some spouses reject institutionalization even when it is the most appropriate source of care; some are grateful for the respite. At the time illness strikes, too few couples are able to benefit from in-depth counseling, because most institutional intake programs lack the professional personnel. An important question to consider is whose needs will be met through institutionalization, whether or not the factors precipitating application are related to crises or long-standing dynamics. In these cases, it is important to observe interactions, to learn about the needs that are expressed therein, and to understand the ways the actions of each person repeatedly influence those of the other.

If both members of an aged couple have functional limitations, or if an aged parent is alone, it is more likely that the middle-aged child, who is beginning to experience his own aging process, will become involved in giving support to the first generation. Support can be given in the form of financial assistance, direct assistance with physical care, or involvement in making important life decisions for the aging parent.

Sometimes old people feel their family does not have time for them. The less invested aged people are in the dynamics of their own lives or the fewer social contacts they have outside the family, the more likely they are to turn to the family as their source of social stimuli. Sometimes the aging process (if general social disengagement has not occurred or if there is no serious depression) brings a blossoming of the older person's interest in the family. The family response to this interest is varied. There are cases where the family does not know how to take this new emotional investment because it is an unfamiliar pattern. If it was not there earlier, adult children used to living without emotional closeness to their aged parents sometimes find it difficult to accept the other person's readiness for intimate social intercourse. Sometimes it cannot occur.

Another area of important interaction is the decision-making process. An aged person who has always been dependent on decisions made by other people can easily accept adult children making these decisions. If the person has a history of independence and is now physically or mentally dependent, the reaction to family involvement can be very negative. Furthermore, if the aged person is becoming increasingly more confused without knowing it, he or she can also react strongly to the family's involvement. Participation in the decision-making process by the aged person and family is critical to the success of any placement in day care centers.[5]

Living Arrangements

In order for day care services to be a successful form of long-term care, there must be a compatible living arrangement. A suitable long-term care community living arrangement must provide an environment adapted to support the individual's functional limitations and, thereby, insure an individual the right to an optimal quality of life.

Participant family members exert an important influence on the aged person's ability to live in the community and make full use of day care services. Clinical data from ongoing day care programs indicate that families perform such important functions as helping the aged person to participate in family roles and activities, helping the aged person to maintain the best possible appearance, monitoring the changes in mental and physical conditions, assuming responsibility for getting the aged person to services outside the day care center, and continuing to support the emotional bonds that are part of family life. Some family members report spending as much as one hour in the morning helping aged members get ready to come to the center; others indicate that work and leisure schedules have had to be rearranged to accommodate the aged member's schedule in the day care program. But it is clear that appropriate day care center services combined with this kind of appropriate, highly supportive living arrangement is an extremely effective form of long-term care.

Data are now available to describe the living arrangements that help sustain the aged person in day care centers. A recently completed survey of 10 day care centers in the United States indicates that of 300 participants, 69 percent lived with other people, including a relative or nonrelative, compared to 31 percent who lived alone.[6] Since the Levindale day care center's beginning in 1970, 79 percent of its participants have lived with relatives.

The importance of the living arrangement and the family unit has been documented by Townsend[7] and by Shanas,[8] who points out that when community services are provided, they supplement rather than substitute for those services provided by the children. Nationally, the majority of aged persons live alone, but there is an increased proportion of persons over 80 who live with family members other than spouses once they become more dependent.[9] This pattern is characteristic of many persons in day care centers.

Data collected from the 1968 Social Security Survey of the demographic and economic characteristics of the aged show many different living arrangements for the aged.[10] It is possible that day care centers can be structured to accommodate aged persons in different living arrangements as long as an appropriate and responsible person is available during nights and weekends.

Family Dynamics

In 1972, extensive data were gathered on 28 participants in the Levindale day care program and on 26 of their closest family members. The participants had been at the center for a minimum of two months. The family data supported the supposition that family members were struggling with the burden of caring for an impaired elderly family member. For these families, the day care arrangement represented a last ditch effort at community maintenance.

Fifty percent of the families indicated that the aged person created some degree of strain on the family unit. This strain was typically associated with emotions rather than finances. All of the families interviewed considered the aged member to be unable to function without family assistance. Families also indicated that they often neglected other family responsibilities in order to provide the required assistance. Seventy-three percent of the families considered the aged member to be either a secondary family member or one who was not fulfilling any social role in the family unit.

While the families reported many common attitudes and problems, the uniqueness of each individual family was revealed through the open-ended portion of the interview and was supplemented by the case history obtained by the clinical social worker at the time of the admission process. Four examples show some of the most important patterns of family dynamics:

Mrs. B. was an 89-year-old widow who had resided with her unmarried daughter for many years. At the time of placement the daughter was considering institutionalizing her mother. Mrs. B. was very dependent physically and emotionally, and was limited in her ability to ambulate, feed, and dress herself. She tended to remain withdrawn from her peers. A second, married daughter lived close-by, but did not participate in the daily care of Mrs. B. The day care program provided the major source of support to reduce the burden of the care-giving daughter. There were indications that the daughter felt that her own personal growth had been inhibited by her mother for many years. Complicating this resentment was an accompanying sense of guilt for thinking of institutional placement.

Mr. S., a 76-year-old man, lived in the home of one of his five children, a married daughter with two children still living at home. He was a poststroke victim, paralyzed and almost completely nonverbal. His daughter suffered from a degenerative disease that placed her own life in question. Throughout Mr. S's three years in the day care program he was subject to episodes of physically disruptive behavior that created a management problem. The daughter consistently indicated that her husband was very supportive of her father; without his active participation, community maintenance would not have been possible. The family was strongly committed to Mr. S's personal well-being.

Mrs. W. was an 80-year-old widow who lived with her daughter and son-in-law. She went to their home after the death of her brother because she had become depressed and could no longer maintain her own apartment. She was institutionalized for a brief period before moving to her daughter's home. At the day care center her jovial manner was a major social influence, but at home she was depressed and apathetic. There was constant conflict between Mrs. W. and the son-in-law, placing the daughter in a tense and awkward position. Mrs. W. became increasingly irritable and paranoid. Despite staff recommendations, the family withdrew her from the program and admitted her to a nursing home. During her stay in the nursing home, she repeatedly pleaded to be allowed to return to day care. The daughter informed Mrs. W. that the day care program had been discontinued. Mrs. W. independently contacted the day care staff to confirm this fact. Upon learning that the program was operating, and that she was not welcome back in her daughter's home, she went into a severe depression and was immediately placed in the state mental hospital.

Mr. B. was 83 years old and lived with his wife, who was 76. He experienced a slow, steady decline. During the two years of his participation in the program, he experienced numerous periods of confusion and became increasingly dependent upon assistance in activities of daily living. The wife's physical burden was great, and children were not available to provide direct assistance because of geographical distance. Were it not for the relief provided by the program, the wife's commitment as care-giver would have been impossible.

It should be noted that there have been cases in both the Levindale and Lexington centers where aged couples have participated in the programs. At times both husband and wife have been equally in need of day care services, but more frequently one has needed the services more than the other. They both come as participants because of tremendous emotional interdependencies. This can create a special set of problems. In these cases, frequently there is a pattern of overdependency throughout marriage and the dependencies of both husband and wife increase with age. During the early phase of their participation, the couple tends to remain isolated from the larger participant group. The more independent person is reluctant to allow staff to provide routine and special services for the impaired mate and attempts to intervene in care-giving functions similar to those he or she provides in the home setting.

To help these couples make the transition, staff must work slowly but consistently to engage each individual in a daily program plan that will provide them with the opportunity to be together as well as apart. Care must be taken, however, lest separate programming create too much of a threat. For example, in one case at Lexington the husband received daily physical therapy that required him to go to another part of the center. During this hour the wife had to become involved with other activities. At first, specialized arts and crafts were tried, but she had no interest and became aggravated when expected to do these activities. Her need was clearly to be more active and do something she considered "useful." Finally, the husband's physical therapy schedule was rearranged so that it took place one hour before lunch. The wife, on request from staff, became involved in helping nonambulatory participants get cleaned up for lunch and into the dining room on time.

A couple admitted to Levindale were both in good physical condition, but the wife was extremely confused and could no longer be left alone without constant supervision. As part of the weekly care plan, the couple was assigned to one of three different participant discussion groups that were divided according to the level of mental functioning. The social worker recognized that the wife was exceedingly dependent upon her husband, but that he seemed to want to find his own stimulation from participation in center activities. She initially assigned the couple to the group of least-oriented participants, explaining to the couple that if either of them wanted to join another group it could be arranged at a later time. After two meetings, the husband asked the social worker if he could in addition attend another group meeting where there was more talking. For a brief time he attended both groups, but gradually dropped the group in which his wife participated and quickly became one of the formal group leaders, but doing so without disruption to his wife.

Service Implications

There are important service implications in the fact that the family plays a critical role in the choice of day care as a long-term care alternative and in the continuing community maintenance of its elderly members. The family must be engaged first as the day care client is in the admission process; once the elderly person becomes a day care participant, ongoing contact with the family must be maintained and appropriate supports offered.

If admission screening is to be conducted effectively, it will require professional skills to assess the applicant's psychosocial functioning. Part of this assessment consists of uncovering the relationships between family members and the aged person in order to determine the appropriateness of geriatric day care. Ideally, the structure of the admission process requires that the worker, the applicant, and the family form a triad. In many cases the levels of impairment or the threatening impact of the admission process can render the aged person unwilling or unable to participate in a dominant role. If the aged person does not become actively engaged, the interpersonal exchange between the family and the worker is even more crucial.

The worker sets the climate and the framework for the clinical evaluation. It is essential that he or she regard the needs of both the family and the patient as being of equal importance. Too frequently,

115

workers perceive simply that the family is to be categorized as a resource either available or not available to the aged person, that there is malfunction in the applicant-family relationship, or that the family is seeking a depository for the aged person. The extent to which the worker can apply the standards of "concerned neutrality" and identify the family as part of the client system helps to assure a more accurate assessment.

Many factors have to be explored in the application process. Briefly summarized, here are some of the most important issues that reflect directly on the family/aged person relationship:

Pattern of the living arrangement:

1. Does the person live with the family member? For how long?
2. What were the circumstances leading to the decision for mutual living? Who initiated the idea?
3. What is the level of satisfaction of each member of the family about the arrangement? (Ask each family member privately.)
4. What would be considered the optimal situation if a number of alternatives were available? Can family members be freed to participate in areas of personal interest and meaningful activity?

Levels of physical care and attention required:

1. What activities of daily living can the aged person do for himself or herself? Does he or she do as much as possible?
2. Which members of the family are available to share in the responsibility of care? What care objectives does the family set for the person?
3. Are the responsibilities equally shared? What are the attitudes?
4. What relief to the family is anticipated through the services of day care?

Financial resources:

1. Can the day care per diem fee be paid?
2. What funds will be used to pay for care?
3. Does the expenditure of funds for day care seem justified in light of the possibility of eventually having to cover the cost of institutional care?
4. Does the aged person represent a financial burden?

5. How do the aged person and the family feel about the need to keep the aged person's cash reserve intact for future use?

The application process could require up to three meetings between the worker and the family. First, there would be a preliminary interview with the family member who is initiating the inquiry; second, a joint visit by the aged person and the family member to see the day care facilities and to let the worker describe the program to the aged person; third, a home visit with all involved family members present. The particular procedure might vary from case to case; however, these steps are important to insure an appropriate placement.

Ideally, admission should be only the first step of intervention with the family. Once the individual is enrolled in the program, there is a need to maintain an ongoing relationship between the service unit and the family (see chapter 8).

Conclusion

Day care services benefit supporting families in three ways:

1. They provide an organized service unit that can share significantly in the complex burden of daily care and supervision of aged persons.

2. They provide psychological support in the knowledge that the aged family member is involved in a social-health environment that fosters supervised peer interaction.

3. They provide a means by which the family is able to fulfill the desire to keep the aged person at home for as long as possible.

One family member eloquently stated the feelings of many:

Eight years ago, when my mother was widowed, she came to live with us. At that time I knew that things would go smoothly because we were a close family and everybody gets along. We love each other. I did dread the thought of how things might be for mother and us when she grew feeble. After her stroke she was forced to reduce her community activities and lost touch with the few friends still alive. Just before I heard about the day care program, I was ready to try placing her in an old age home as she was so depressed and unhappy and I couldn't get her interested in anything. After a few months in the program, she was a different person and I was greatly relieved.

Notes

1. Alvin I. Goldfarb, "Psychodynamics and the Three Generational Family," and Marvin B. Sussman, "Relationships of Adult Children with Parents in the United States," in Ethel Shanas and Gordon Streib, eds., *Social Structure and the Family* (Englewood Cliffs, N.J.: Prentice Hall, 1965); Eugene Litwork, "Geographical Mobility and Extended Family Cohesion," *American Sociological Review,* vol. 25, no. 3, 1960, pp. 385–394; Marvin B. Sussman and Lee Burchinal, "Kin Network: Unheralded Structure in Current Conceptualization of Family Functioning," *Marriage and Family Living,* vol. 24, no. 3, 1962, pp. 231–240.

2. Bertha G. Simos, "Adult Children and Their Aging Parents," *Social Work,* vol. 18, no. 3, May 1973, pp. 78–85.

3. Edna Wasser, *Creative Approach in Casework with the Aging* (New York: Family Service Association of America, 1960), p. 36.

4. Elaine Brody and Geraldine Spark, "Institutionalization of the Aged: A Family Crisis," *Family Process,* vol. 21, March 1966, pp. 76–90.

5. Elaine M. Brody, "Long-Term Care: The Decision-Making Process and Individual Assessment," *Human Factors in Long-Term Health Care,* Final Report of the Task Force, National Conference on Social Welfare, June 1975, pp. 33–59.

6. William Weissert, *Adult Day Care in the U.S.: A Comparative Study,* final report funded by contract #HRA-B6-74-148 (Rockville, Md.: National Center for Health Services Research, Health Resources Administration, Public Health Service, Department of Health, Education, and Welfare, 1975).

7. Peter Townsend, *The Last Refuge* (London: Routledge and Kegan Paul, 1962).

8. Ethel Shanas, "Measuring the Home Health Needs of the Aged in Four Countries," paper presented at the 8th International Congress of Gerontology, Washington, D.C., August 1969.

9. Janet Murray, "Living Arrangements of People Aged 65 and Older: Findings from 1968 Survey of the Aged," *Social Service Bulletin,* vol. 34, no. 9, September 1971, pp. 3–14.

10. Ibid.

10

Reimbursement and Fiscal Management

Introduction

The importance of funding and reimbursement for day care services is self-evident. Without a method of financing the services, all that is now being done will stop and all that is planned for the future will not occur. Centers are not likely to be developed, continue to operate, or receive third-party reimbursement if fiscal management does not reflect efforts to control costs. If the initial dollar investment required for start-up is too great, many potential providers will choose not to offer the service. If the cost incurred by the older person or the family is too great, another service alternative will be selected or they will elect to do without. Finally, if the cost of day care is not lower than or, at most, equal to the cost of 24-hour inpatient care, third-party agents will strongly resist offering financial coverage.

Following is a discussion of the federal entitlements currently used to fund day care centers, and a discussion of several other important aspects of fiscal management, including budget development, start-up costs, auditing and accounting, purchase and supply, and cost-effectiveness.

Reimbursement—An Overview

Several years ago, when only a few day care centers were being established, the primary impetus for growth resulted from interaction between a limited number of agencies within DHEW and the local organizations that had received federal research and demonstration grants. In addition, limited funding has been available through Title III of the Older Americans Act and through private funding sources (see chapter 4). At present, a few experimental day care centers continue to be funded by federal, state, or private grants, but the majority of new and old programs are struggling with the issues related to third-party reimbursement. Titles XVIII (Medicare, 1965), XIX (Medicaid, 1965), and XX (of the 1975 amendments to the Social Security Act) are now providing a source of reimbursement for a limited number of day care centers, and there will be an increasing effort to use these entitlements as more centers begin to develop throughout the United States.

Tracing the historical development of the aforementioned entitlements, it is possible to identify a trend toward greater state involvement as the federal government has made a concentrated effort to decentralize the human services bureaucracy. In 1976, we find state involvement dominant in both Titles XIX and XX; if the current trend continues, it can be anticipated that states will also have a greater involvement in Title XVIII. This means that in the future the states will have a greater amount of authority and a well-established link with the federal level regarding resource allocations for health and medical care. Those individuals who seek reimbursement for their organization's services will not be making the routine pilgrimage to the regional Medicare office to gain access to these funds. The power will have been diverted to the states.

Title XX Funding

The new Title XX is a federal policy, but the states are charged with the responsibility for allocating these funds according to their own priorities. Upon notification by the states of these priorities, the social service provider system must assume the responsibility for developing programs that fit into these priorities.

According to federal policy, states may use Title XX funds in pursuit of five basic goals:

1. to help people become or remain economically self-supporting,

2. to help people become or remain self-sufficient,

3. to protect children and adults who cannot protect themselves from abuse, neglect, and exploitation, and to help families stay together,

4. to prevent and reduce inappropriate institutional care as much as possible by making home and community services available,

5. to arrange for appropriate placement and services in an institution when this is in an individual's best interest.

By examining Maryland's broad experience it is possible to understand how Title XX can be used for the reimbursement of geriatric day care services in all states. The description of the Maryland experience highlights both the positive and negative aspects of linking day care services to Title XX.

In fiscal year 1973, the governor of the state of Maryland signed into law a bill to provide for the establishment of day care centers for the elderly. These centers were intended to give aged persons the opportunity to remain with their families and in their communities, rather than being placed in nursing homes or state institutions, to allow families to keep their elderly parents and relatives with them, and to allow the state to deal more effectively and economically with the needs of its elderly citizens. Further, the bill authorized the Maryland State Department of Health and Mental Hygiene and the Department of Employment and Social Services to negotiate the purchase of day care services for the elderly from public and private agencies.

Prior to and in conjunction with the efforts to get this legislation passed, a state plan was developed to create a comprehensive service system for the aged. This plan included day care services as one of several institutional alternatives. A consortium of state officials worked to make it both broad enough and feasible enough to be implementable, and included a projection of future services to fit existing reimbursement sources.

To capitalize on Titles XVIII, XIX, and VI (1935 amendments to the Social Security Act), it was necessary to propose levels of day care that would vary according to the mixture of health and social services. As proposed, the day hospital would provide direct medical care and try to serve those with acute and chronic conditions so that Title XVIII could be used for service reimbursement. The adult day treatment center was to provide a strong health component with related social service supports for aged persons in need of intermediate or skilled care; Title XIX was a potential source of reimbursement for this group.

Title VI was to be used for day care centers for the elderly, which were designed to provide the much-needed protective environment for those aged persons at risk of premature institutionalization. This strategy was developed by a cadre of administrators from several state agencies and concerned community and professional representatives. It was supported by necessary legislative action and placed Maryland in a unique position to move rationally and swiftly toward the goal of a statewide network of day care services. In October, 1975, Title XX replaced Title VI, making it necessary to insure that some portion of Title XX funds could be used for day care center services for the elderly. The Maryland state legislature authorized this.

Title XX offers a 75/25 match between federal and state funds and requires that at least 50 percent go for services to low-income individuals and recipients of Aid to Families with Dependent Children, Social Security Insurance, and/or Medicaid. In addition, state service goals developed as part of the state plan must be compatible with the five previously stated federal goals. The Maryland Office on Aging made $150,000 available in state monies, which represented the 25 percent match monies required to obtain Title XX funds for adult day care, and this enabled a contractual arrangement to be developed for the delivery of day care services between February 1, 1975, and January 31, 1976.

As of July, 1976, Title XX funds have been awarded to six organizations in Maryland, based on a competitive grant review process rather than the originally proposed contractual arrangements. This change was very important to help insure the quality of these experimental day care centers and eliminate the tendency to award to the lowest bidder without regard to quality of service. Settings defined as eligible to submit grant proposals had to have established relationships with local health and social agencies and proven management capabilities. Inpatient facilities providing primarily custodial services or those having significant deficiencies were not eligible to submit a proposal for a day care center.

An interdepartmental review committee, which will continue for the foreseeable future, was formed to evaluate the applications. There is unanimous agreement that the continuation of this committee is essential to insure that the necessary expertise is available and that this committee has the authority to carry out its mandate. So far, Maryland has done an effective job of utilizing Title XX for the growth of day care services.

As not all six centers have begun operation, there is a limited base on which to evaluate the impact of Title XX. On the other hand, several crucial problems have already become evident and warrant consideration. At the present time, those responsible for intake at the centers are screening applications and considering the acceptance of some persons who have not yet been determined to be eligible for Title XX. These workers are sending applications to be processed by local departments of social service by personnel who are not yet familiar with the highly complex process of eligibility determination. (The law was changed in January, 1976, to increase the time for eligibility determination from 10 to 30 days.)

Center personnel are now admitting people who will be dropped from the program if they are found to be ineligible. Staff find themselves in a serious dilemma and helpless to alter the situation unless they defer applications of those in immediate need of the services. As usual, the aged are caught in the middle. The majority of people ready to be admitted to these centers are at risk. A 30-day delay between application and actual admission can mean the difference between the individual's successful or unsuccessful effort to remain in the community.

For now, these centers are locked into the requirements of Title XX. In the future, there is a possibility of greater flexibility, but even then day care participants will have to be within a given financial range; no provisions have been made for financing ineligible applicants. It is hoped that some monies beyond what has been made available as matching funds can be found for this purpose.

Another glaring problem with Title XX is the limitation it places on the health care component of the centers. These programs are not allowed to provide direct health care. A nurse may be hired as the program coordinator and health consultants may be used extensively, but this is not a substitute for direct health services. Some centers are trying to provide health care to participants on a fee-for-service basis from Medicaid at health facilities located near the center. It is still too early to determine how successfully this strategy will work. However, no day care center proposing to provide an alternative to institutionalization should be without a strong health component. The problems of eligibility and the restrictions on health services raise serious questions about the long-range viability of Title XX as a major source of reimbursement for day care.

Title XIX (Medicaid) Funding

Levindale's day care program unintentionally became the test case for obtaining Medicaid as a reimbursement source for day care. From July 1, 1970, when the day care center began operation, until late in 1973, the program was funded primarily by a demonstration grant awarded by the Maryland State Commission on Aging. Originally, the grant was to last for three years, but an extension of six months was obtained to ease the transition from grant-based to third-party funding. Although the Levindale grant funds came through a state grant rather than a federal grant, the process of shifting from grant-based to third-party reimbursement will be similar for all programs, regardless of the source of their grant funds.

Levindale's decision was to attempt to secure Medicaid reimbursement through existing mechanisms and not through the standard Medicaid 1115 waiver, which allows for special reimbursement for demonstration projects and/or geographically defined variations in benefits and reimbursement methods. This decision was predicated on the certainty that many of the day care participants were eligible for intermediate and/or skilled care and that some met the financial eligibility requirement. To conform to the state's plan for multiple levels of geriatric day care, Levindale changed the name of the program to Adult Day Treatment Center; this did not represent any shift in the proportion of health and social services, since the necessary health services had been there since 1970.

When Levindale's first contacts were initiated with the Director of Medical Policy for Medicaid, geriatric day care was a new concept and not readily understood by Medicaid officials. Medicaid did not (and still does not) have any guidelines for covering day care services. To give evidence of the population's eligibility, all participants were requested to have their private physician complete the medical form that is used to determine eligibility. The results proved the point. Over 50 percent were medically eligible for intermediate or skilled nursing care and one-third were financially eligible.

An important dimension of the transfer from grant to third-party reimbursement was the experience of the aged person and his family. It should be noted that Levindale's day care population is comprised of people with middle-class backgrounds. They perceive Medicaid, unlike Medicare, to be charity. Unless a person has been on Medicaid prior to coming to the program, to be confronted with having to make application to Medicaid to be accepted into the program is a troubling experience.

The method currently used by Medicaid for reimbursing the day care center is not considered to be satisfactory for the institution's need. Medicaid does not pay the full cost of care; it pays only a negotiated rate for those expenses Medicaid can afford, on the grounds that its budget is limited for this type of special service funding. Further, the rate only covers those days participants actually attend the program. This could bankrupt a program, because the attendance is not always predictable. The program must continue to operate all services as though attendance were 100 percent, even though Medicaid is not reimbursing them.

Reimbursement Limitations

Some important generalizations can be made about Titles XIX and XX as funding sources and about the administrative demands that accompany reimbursement. The broadest generalization is that while both sources of reimbursement are appropriate for covering the cost of day care, neither reimbursement source is without limitations.

For example, there is a trend throughout the country for the costs of Medicaid programs to increase. Thus, in an effort to minimize the deficits, many states are reducing the range of services covered under Medical Assistance, are undertaking major reevaluations of current expenditures and program coverage, and are avoiding pressure to expand reimbursement to cover additional service areas. Long-term care services are a major expense, and there is concern to try to control costs while at the same time upgrading the quality of service. Cutbacks that seriously affect the elderly are now being enacted. Noninstitutional long-term care services are considered to be important, but there is much hesitancy about committing funds to cover these new programs. Day care services are but one example of services that are being proposed and developed without assurance that Medicaid funds will be available. Likelihood of coverage is even further reduced when the service emphasis is not clearly medical.

Some proponents of day care are suggesting that Title XX funds are the single most appropriate source of funding because of the liberal federal/state funding ratio. The federal government will pay for 75 percent of all services aimed at one of the five basic service goals up to each state's allocation limit. Several states have designated that a noninstitutional long-term care program is to be part of the state plan, and day care programs have been specified in some state plans. Maryland is one of those states and, therefore, has been able to capitalize on Title XX funds to expand the scope of day care. Perhaps the single greatest limitation of Title XX is the eligibility process, as states must devise methods for determining eligibility on an individual basis using a means test. After March 31, 1976, states were no longer allowed to use a group eligibility approach. Staff and administrators now report that the demands for eligibility determination are too complex and time consuming, and that a means-test approach is dehumanizing and alienating for the elderly.

In Kentucky, a research and demonstration project is presently experimenting with the provision of day care services through a standard Medicaid 1115 waiver regulation. This waiver was obtained through the state Medical Assistance Agency and the regional office of DHEW. This effort was authorized by P.L. 92–603, Section 222, which also permits experimental waivers of Medicare regulations to allow payment for adult day care services. These waivers do not provide, at present, any stable long-term funding basis for day care.

The administrator of a day care program must ultimately assume the leadership in obtaining third-party reimbursement. Therefore, if this type of funding is considered to be important for the development and continuation of day care programs, an administrator must be prepared to handle negotiations with state and local officials while recognizing that, once standards for day care are firmly established, considerable time and energy will need to be devoted to insuring that the center continually maintains service standards and fulfills accountability requirements for continued reimbursement.

Fiscal Management

Assuming that the initial and ongoing problems of reimbursement are dealt with satisfactorily, there are several other aspects of fiscal management with which the day care administration must be concerned. Although there is no one best approach to the equitable allocation of program resources, this administrative function is important throughout all stages of programming. Through a series of trials and errors, each administrator will eventually settle upon the approach that best accommodates the phenomenon of the scarcity of resources to be distributed among too many people. The harsh reality of scarce program resources is a familiar situation in the delivery of services. Yet, if a center is to operate efficiently and effectively, there must be a plan of fiscal management that embraces program objectives and functions. The cost of errors that arise from faulty decision-making about budgets can be devastating for the program.

Fiscal management is concerned with accounting, auditing, and the procurement of equipment and supplies. It is important in the operation of a day care center because financial resources must be distributed in a rational manner to insure that the specific program needs of the participants are adequately met. Decisions about distribution require an identification of actual and potential sources of program support as well as a specification of the broad and specific program objectives.

127

Budget Development

Administrative operation of a day care center also entails decision making about budget that assigns fiscal priorities to functional program costs such as personnel, supplies, medical care, health-related care, and transportation. While development (by a step-down accounting method) of the costs and their constituent elements can be expected to vary among types of centers, the following cost categories are common to most centers: general administration, nutritional services, health care services, supportive health care services, and transportation services.[1]

General administration costs include items supportive to overall program functioning: clerical and maintenance personnel, financial and medical record-keeping, direct service personnel, plant operations (utilities, insurance, in-service training, research), and building fixtures. Beyond the initial program costs, costs for general administration can be expected to account for somewhere between 15 and 20 percent of the total operating budget.

Nutrition, in the authors' opinion, needs to be a separate cost item because of its importance not only to program operation but also to the health and well-being of the program participants. Given the expected variability of participants' dietary needs, costs for food services are around 10 percent of the program budget. This estimate includes, in addition to the cost for individual meals, costs for their planning and preparation. It must be emphasized that this is one budget category that should not be compromised; any program that provides meals to its participants must assure their nutritional adequacy.

Health care costs, in general, encompass all services directed toward the medical care needs of the program participants. Minimally, they should include health care supervision and the most basic nursing services. In addition, and again allowing for program variation, they might include separate costing for physicians, pharmacy, psychologists, psychiatrists, and such specialized therapy as physical, occupational, speech, and hearing. The outlay for medical services should be expected to range from 20 to 25 percent of the total operating budget.

Supportive health care costs can be differentiated from health care costs in that the former are incurred as a result of nonmedical services, whereas the latter are a result of direct medical care intervention. This dichotomy is not intended to establish a hierarchy of importance; rather, it identifies a budgetary framework within which fiscal management can operate. Thus, for budgetary purposes, supportive health care costs include such items as nurses aides, social work and social services, arts and crafts therapy, socialization therapy, religious counseling, reality therapy, patient assistance, intake, and admission.

As with the other identified program costs, costs for supportive health care will vary with differing program formats and service emphases, and will account for 40 to 45 percent of the total program operating budget.

Transportation, the final program cost, is optional, depending on the level of support and the nature and scope of program services. Research on transportation services in a day care program operation indicates that transportation can be expected to account for 15 to 20 percent of the total budget.[2] This figure is based on the center's budgetary data on transportation costs supplied through a variety of alternatives, such as private carriers, contracted services, and program-oriented transportation systems; it also includes the cost of vehicle maintenance and upkeep. On the other hand, for a day care program to operate without incurring transportation costs per se, a great deal of planning and coordination will still be needed before the program opens. This might include the planning and coordination of voluntary motor pools, lobbying for the rerouting of public transportation, or requiring program participants to provide their own transportation. Any strategy will result in a direct cost outlay from the program budget, but depending on the characteristics of the program one method of transportation may be more cost-efficient than the other.

To summarize, the development of a budget through the identification of major costs offers the administrator a framework within which to operate fiscally, and provides a perspective for allocating resources according to service priorities. In addition, when such a budget development is maintained throughout the project's life, the administrator has a ready-made scheme for periodic evaluation of the program's effect or, when it terminates, its outcome.

Cost Consideration

Start-up costs, cost projection (both short-run and long-run), cost containment, and cost-effectiveness are also important issues in program development.

Start-up costs are for those ancillary resources necessary for a program actually to become operational. They can be incurred through such activities as site location, licensure and certification determination, structural modifications and alterations, interagency coordination and integration, public relations, staff recruitment, definition of program goals, establishment of admission/discharge criteria, determination of the scope and nature of program services, reimbursement qualifications and potentials, and population identification and description. The list could go on, but the point is that there are a host of potentially costly activities that demand administrative consideration prior to actual program operation.[3]

Currently, variation in the amounts required for start-up costs has been a function of whether the center site is free standing or attached to an existing institution. With a free-standing facility, the option for reliance on existing physical structures is often closed; the proposed treatment program must, in essence, begin from the ground and work up. On the other hand, in the case of an attached setting, the administrative mechanisms and supportive services such as maintenance, record-keeping, utilities, and the like may already be in place. One can logically expect that the start-up costs for such an attached program will be less than for a free-standing situation.

Cost projection of any accuracy may prove to be very difficult during the early stages of the program operation. Basically, there are two levels of cost projections: short-term and long-term. Most, if not all, treatment programs will be faced with finite, time-limited resources, the majority of which are now in the form of state and/or federal research and demonstration monies. These funding sources often do not afford staff the opportunities for looking beyond the terminal date of the grant cycle and, as a consequence, fiscal management has a short-term time perspective. Nevertheless, even when operating within these fiscal constraints, program management should operate in an atmosphere of optimism not only with an eye toward day-to-day operations but also within the context of securing the continuation of the program over time. Flexibility can be built into this latter aspect of fiscal management by evaluating, in the early stages of program operations, alternative funding sources and potentials that could conceivably support, sustain, and broaden the financial base of the program in the future. A number of alternatives have been addressed at length in chapter 4. It has been the experience of the authors that the most frequent impediment to the continued operation of day care centers for the elderly has been the absence of long-range fiscal management and planning. The sooner program personnel, particularly the project administrator, realize that they, too, will be competing for scarce resources, the greater will be their chance for securing operating funds for the future. Both short-range and long-range fiscal management cannot begin too soon.

Cost containment is as important in fiscal management as cost projection. Failure to place an upper limit on a unit charge per service may encourage certain segments of the elderly population to look elsewhere for more comprehensive services at the same cost. By not placing a lower limit on these same service units, the program runs the risk of alienating or disallowing potential and current sources of external program support. This dilemma is familiar in the field of health care delivery today and it threatens to loom even larger tomorrow. There are no ready answers, either. No program can be expected to be isolated from the current market forces of inflation, higher wage demands, the increasing costs of equipment and operation, and competition for patients and resources from other forms of health service delivery. Nevertheless, operating on principles of sound fiscal management can insure the life of any program to the extent that services are being delivered efficiently, effectively, and competitively to the population in need.

One method for gauging cost containment is to compare the per diem costs of hospital care and nursing home care to the per diem costs of day care. It should also be recognized that the broader objective of day care is not to replace the current dominance of long-term care institutions but to provide an alternative form of care that supports and enhances the elderly person's living arrangement in the community.

Within the context of fiscal management, cost-effectiveness analytical strategies offer an alternative for enhancing both the quantity and quality of care service delivery to the elderly. Quantitatively, given fixed resources, cost/effect ratios allow for the determination of service type and scope. Qualitatively, these techniques offer a method for insuring that the services being delivered are, in fact, resulting in some gains for the recipients. While most often utilized after the program is operational, these tools are indispensable for assuring that the program is functioning within the mandated guidelines of both cost and services.

Conclusion

Fiscal management is but one of a series of procedures through which services are delivered to the elderly. Its purpose is to facilitate, through proper accounting, auditing, and procurement, the achievement of the overall program objectives. It aids the development of a functional program budget through the delineation of various major program costs, and thus insures against the overspending and maldistribution of program resources that hamper ongoing program activities. Finally, fiscal management heightens the visibility of those program issues that can be expected to have an impact, both in the short-run and the long-run, on the continued operation of a day care center. Adherence to sound fiscal management principles and practices does not guarantee the longevity of any health care delivery system, nor does it guarantee that, once the services are in place, the program will continue to operate smoothly. However, their use does increase the probability that those in need of services will receive them and that the services will be delivered in a timely, economical, and effective manner.

Notes

1. Nicholas Dopuch, J. Bernberg, and Joel Demski, *Cost Accounting: Data for Management's Decisions* (New York: Harcourt Brace Jovanovich, 1974), p. 582. This includes an explanation of the step-down accounting method.

2. Nevill Doherty et al., *Cost-Benefit Analysis of Alternative Care Programs for the Elderly,* paper presented at the 28th Annual Scientific meeting of the American Gerontological Society, Louisville, Ky., October 1975.

3. Helen Padula, *Developing Day Care for Older People* (Washington, D.C.: The National Council on the Aging, September 1972).

11

Review of Day Care Research

Program Evaluation

Program evaluation, and particularly evaluation of a health and social service program such as adult day care, can be defined as a social process of measuring the degree to which ongoing service programs achieve stated program goals, of judging the outcomes of the service program, and of documenting the rationale of program expansion, maintenance, modification, or discontinuation.

To date, all federally funded adult day care center demonstration projects have required an evaluation component. Their research activities have proved difficult and complex. The majority of studies have attempted to address one of the following program areas: effectiveness, costs, and policy.

Program Effectiveness

This analysis attempts to evaluate the health and functional status of patients during a certain time period, and is measured in terms of patient outcomes. Although effectiveness is one of the most crucial issues to determine in any evaluation of day care, it is one of the most difficult. The first problem is that there is no widely accepted good instrument to use for the functional assessment of the patients. Most studies use a combination of existing instruments[1] or develop new ones.

134

Whether using a validated or a specially developed research instrument, program evaluators should be sensitive to validity and reliability, which are always relative and situational, since they depend on research setting and, particularly, on sample subjects. Invalid and/or unreliable instruments are counterproductive, not only for decision making about the program, but for comparisons of data in the general body of knowledge about the welfare of the elderly.

A clear understanding of how the elderly interpret and respond to questionnaires and similar data-gathering instruments has not been well delineated. The response styles of elderly research subjects are not well known. This may produce significant bias in the data.

Another problem in evaluating program effectiveness is the determination of appropriate comparison and control groups. Few studies have defined adequate control groups that are either randomly selected or are matched with the study group. However, administrative and program procedures may prevent the random assignment of patients to experimental and control groups, adequate populations may not be available, and the cost and time factors involved in implementing this design may be prohibitive. Some agencies have developed a Human Subjects Review Committee that carefully screens all research to determine the potential consequences for the well-being of clients. These committees can significantly influence the type of program evaluation to be undertaken. It may be difficult for either the participants or Human Subjects Review Committee to agree to such a methodology.

The evaluation component of the long-term care projects authorized by P.L. 92–603, Section 222, requires of all projects a standardized form of sample selection.[2] In these studies, clients are randomly assigned to experimental and control groups. The experimental group receives the expanded benefit of day care services and the control group does not. These services may or may not be utilized by the experimental patients. Implementation of sample selection procedures has proved to be difficult because clients want access to the services of their choice, and the general community has responded negatively when it perceives that services are being withheld in order to conduct research.

Other types of comparison methods have been employed in day care evaluations. For instance:

1. Participant group: The participants are their own control, being evaluated before, during, and after receiving program services. This format is not rigorous, and fails to account for what the participants would have done without the program.

2. "Comparable" community group: Several studies (e.g., the Triage project[3]) use this approach, but it is difficult to obtain an adequate matched sample without introducing unknown biases. Furthermore, with this type of control one must determine whether the institutionalized aged should be included. Finally, to consider day care as an alternative to institutional care implies that one can substitute one for the other. This is not the case. Day care is an option for those inappropriately institutionalized.

3. Community-based data on morbidity and service utilization patterns for the aged: This method has severe limitations because of its lack of specificity.

4. Optimum allocation method: This method attempts to obtain a sample with randomly distributed characteristics in the total population.

The time limitation to study program effectiveness in most studies is also problematic. The pressure for quick research results and immediacy of decision making serve to shorten the time allowed to conduct evaluations. Short-term research fails to account for the long-term impact of services and, thus, measures of program impact are weakened.

Finally, though attempting to quantify program effectiveness, evaluations should not fail to reflect some of the qualitative aspects or effects of the program. Qualitative data are invaluable for the accurate interpretation of results and further program planning. Staff observations and client experience are excellent sources of descriptive information. Day care evaluations are greatly enhanced by the selective synthesis of qualitative and quantitative data about client outcomes.

Program Costs

This focuses on analysis of direct and indirect provider costs in delivering day care services. A step-down accounting technique (see chapter 10) is appropriate and insures a comparison of the direct and indirect costs associated with major cost centers. Factors that should be considered in any cost analysis of service delivery are:

1. 24-hour costs or total life maintenance costs,
2. costs of other services used to support the patient in the community,
3. public costs (Medicare, Medicaid, welfare programs, etc.) vs. private costs (private income of patient, family, friends),
4. costs for patterns of service utilization (doctor's visits, hospital admissions, nursing home admissions, etc.).

Patient diaries maintained by the patients and/or their families have not proved to be satisfactory in reflecting these costs. Other costs that may be considered are opportunity costs (revenue lost as a result of a service being or not being utilized) and sunk costs (costs already invested in another system that become an obstacle to that system's being abandoned or changed).

Program Policy

Evaluation results should be relevant to the appropriateness of day care in the long-term continuum. A wide range of factors must be considered in the evaluation for the formulation of policies about day care service delivery. Two of the most important are what role the service will play in publicly financed health care programs and how day care centers will be integrated into existing human services systems.

Program policy analysis also examines the extent to which programs meet their service objectives. These objectives have to be stated clearly in measurable terms to permit valid evaluation. The objectives usually include the following areas:

1. cost effectiveness of day care compared to that of institutional settings,
2. effectiveness of day care services in preparing the institutionalized patient for early release to his or her home and/or for a more independent living arrangement in the community,
3. ability of day care to prevent the institutionalization of the elderly at risk,
4. ability of day care to provide sufficient support and relief to families so that those who wish to do so can keep the elderly person at home,

5. ability of day care to offer a more humane and satisfying method of caring for the problems of the elderly than do traditional institutional settings.

Other objectives may be stated for the programs, and should be evaluated to determine program effect. These objectives can be community-oriented (such as in the Lexington program) or directed toward such specific aspects of aging as drug use, senility, and adult abuse.

Other issues are relevant for policy formulation but remain only partly answered:

1. Monitoring of the quality of care and appropriate utilization of the mix of services in day care centers has not been adequately clarified. Current professional review and quality control methods are not well adapted for use in day care centers.[4] The most appropriate patient mix for day care also needs to be further analyzed (e.g., the ratio of wheelchair to ambulatory patients, disoriented to oriented patients, older to younger patients).

2. Significant program variables (such services as health, nursing, socialization, nutrition, and recreation) that affect the predescribed program outcome have to be analyzed to determine their relative value. Day care studies have tended to rely on traditional patterns of data analysis and most frequently include two variable relationships. Significant methodological advances will be made when a greater number of evaluation research designs consider a multivariable interaction to maximize a description of the phenomena under investigation. By analyzing all interrelated variables that affect the conditions of the elderly, we should be better able to understand the parameters of their problems and consequently better able to develop more comprehensive intervention programs.

It appears worthwhile for further research activities of this type to include a causal pattern analysis. This type of analysis is efficient and is sometimes classified as a form of multivariate analysis. Some social science methodologists have indicated that this is the only tool available for describing a causal relationship among numerous variables, and that it would help determine the most significant variables influencing program outcome. This would strengthen program variables that contribute to the success of the program while controlling adverse program variables.[5] In order to utilize this causal pattern analysis appropriately, however, a minimum of 100 sample subjects is strongly recommended.

3. Furthermore, such issues as the ratio of professional to para-professional staff and the ratio of staff to patients have not been sufficiently evaluated by time-flow analyses, comparative studies of different centers, or other methods.

Program Planning

More research is needed to define adequately the population at risk so that policies can be formulated about the number of day care facilities and patient-days needed. This is essential for any national, state, or local plans that should be developed for such organizations as Health System Agencies or governmental agencies on aging.

To date, the planning for day care has been based on formulas such as those used in England,[6] which are derived from use, demand for services, or felt need. Other planning has been based on estimates from data on different types of broad community studies showing that various percentages of the elderly can be defined as functionally impaired and as prime candidates for community health services.[7]

Research Projects

The experience of certain federally funded projects offers a good overview of current day care research efforts.

Levindale's Research and Evaluation Activities

The first study of the Levindale Adult Treatment Center was completed during 1971–1972.[8] It used an experimental research design that involved experimental and control groups and a comparative analysis of these two groups, and measured ability to perform activities of daily living, motivation for independent functioning, life satisfaction, social role ego-involvement, social role satisfaction, levels of social role involvement, and family attitudes and behavioral patterns. The instrument was compiled by the center staff from various sources. The study tested relationships between Levindale hospital inpatients (the control group) and 28 day care participants (the experimental group). Subjects were matched on a case-by-case basis for general physical health, sex, ethnic background, and general capacity to perform activities of daily living. Data were collected primarily through participant observation and interview.

The study found that the experimental group showed: more involvement in social roles than the control group, greater satisfaction in social roles than the control group, greater life satisfaction than the control group, more involvement in family-related social roles than the control group. It was found that the adult day care program enhanced the participant's resocialization process. Healthy group dynamics as well as the individual participant's self-reliance and independence were clearly visible in the day care group. The study strongly recommended that the adult day care program be considered as an alternative to institutional care for those elderly people who did not require 24-hour care. It was additionally recommended that the concept of resocialization be the paramount principle of all service programs in order to assist elderly people in maintaining their life in the community rather than in an institution.

At the same time as this small scale project was completed, a three-year research and demonstration grant was awarded to the Levindale Hebrew Geriatric Center and Hospital by the Administration on Aging, Office of Human Development, DHEW, effective October, 1972. It was to demonstrate and evaluate the feasibility and cost effectiveness of providing day care services for the elderly in a center, as an alternative to nursing homes and other long-term institutional settings, to evaluate such a program's potential for replicability in other settings, and to suggest legislative changes in benefits to be included in Medicare and Medicaid. Accordingly, the primary objectives of the Levindale research were: to develop and assess service activities to help disabled elderly in the community, to assess the roles and effectiveness of various professional services, to determine patient criteria for day care services, and to explore different models of day care centers.[9]

One hundred and seventy-five sample subjects were selected from four populations: the day care center, the inpatient sector, the community, and apartment dwellers. The experimental group consisted of the 46 day care participants who had enrolled in the day care program during a specific time period. The institutional group consisted of 26 participants randomly selected from the patients of the Levindale Hebrew Geriatric Center and Hospital. The community group of 49 was randomly selected from those who maintained service contact with the Jewish Family and Children's Services, and the group of 54 apartment dwellers was from those living in the Concord Apartment House.

The research instrument, compiled and edited by the research staff at the Levindale Geriatric Research Center, was designed to collect the following information: demographic characteristics; functional health status; service satisfaction; and levels of self-maintenance, independence, and impairment. All but one, the service satisfaction scale, were already available for research use. Six times during the 20-month period, subjects in all four groups were evaluated by research staff using functional health scales that included measurement of physical health, mental health, activities of daily living, and service utilization patterns. Information on demographic characteristics, service satisfaction level, life satisfaction level, self-maintenance and behavioral independence levels, and physical and mental impairment evaluation (PAMIE) were collected twice, at the onset of the study (Time 1) and about one year later (Time 4).

The study produced an avalanche of data too great to be summarized in this section. Nevertheless, a summary percentage comparison of program effects is presented in Table 11.1.

Percentage of effectiveness is computed by adding the percentages of the "improved" and "maintained" effects. Based on these data, the community service setting is empirically documented as most cost effective, while the institutional service setting is shown to be the least cost effective among the four service settings under study.

Table 11.2 shows a comparison of institutional and day care center cost effectiveness that was completed separately. This comparison is based on the per diem cost of care (8 hours of day care and 24 hours of institutional services). In this comparison, day care was more effective than institutional care; the effectiveness/cost ratio is almost five to one.

The three major conclusions of this evaluative study are:

1. Compared to total life-maintenance costs (24 hours a day) and similar service packages, day care is a preferable alternative for the care of the chronically ill and impaired elderly.

2. Cost-effectiveness ratios based on per diem program rates indicate that day care is a preferable alternative to institutional care.

3. From the standpoint of both absolute and relative cost to the public and private sector, day care is the less expensive method of delivering long-term care.

In addition to the above conclusions, the study presented the most important ramifications of day care programming with respect to human values:

1. Day care is one of many potential service innovations that can provide the aged and their families with an optional means of receiving long-term care services.

2. Day care is a setting very conducive to integrating the social and health service components of long-term care in such a way as to maximize the benefits of each.

Table 11.1 Levindale Geriatric Research Study: Participants' Status and Cost Effectiveness

Participants' Status in Each Program (Percent)				
Status	Day Care	Institution	Community	Concord
Improved	44%	7%	21%	0%
Maintained	50	25	42	52
Regressed	6	68	37	48

Cost Effectiveness of Service Environment (24-Hour Cost)			
Service Setting	Effectiveness	Cost	Effectiveness/ Cost*
Day care	94%	$24.00	3.78
Institution	32%	$24.70	1.30
Community	63%	$10.50	6.00
Concord	52%	$12.55	4.14

*McCuan et al. provide a detailed description of the cost effectiveness methodology in the final project report.[10]

Table 11.2   Cost Effectiveness of Day Care and
            Institutional Care

Service Setting	Effectiveness	Cost	Effectiveness/Cost[*]
Day care	94%	$17.02	5.53
Institution	32%	$24.70	1.30

[*]See note to Table 11.1.

3. Day care is a service that is potentially flexible enough to be used with other personal and professional care resources available to the individual.

4. Day care is a realistic means of providing the much-needed support to families wishing to provide care for their elderly family members.

5. Day care is a service vehicle for neutralizing the destructive impact of chronic diseases and impairments, as it allows the aged person to be maintained in a living arrangement outside an institutional setting.

Lexington's Research and Evaluation Activities

The evolution of research and evaluation activities undertaken in conjunction with the Lexington Center for Creative Living (CCL) parallels the pattern at Levindale. The Lexington-Fayette County Health Department initiated evaluation activities in the early stages of program development and, after completion of a small scale evaluation,[11] was awarded a research and demonstration grant effective July, 1974, by the Division of Long Term Care, Health Resources Administration, National Center for Health Services Research, Public Health Service, DHEW.

The initial project was conducted by research staff of the health department during a six-month period beginning in November, 1973, for the first research cycle. The purpose of the study was to determine the degree of accomplishment of the stated program objectives (see chapter 4).

Like the On Lok study discussed later, the CCL evaluation had two groups, experimental and control, that were closely matched with respect to demographic characteristics, initial levels of social and behavioral functioning, and initial mental and physical health conditions. The experimental group consisted of all 31 participants in the initial CCL program. The control group consisted of 35 elderly persons living in the community, all of whom were qualified for CCL services but were on a waiting list because of the small size of the center. At the final stage of the first research cycle, however, there were 25 and 28 participants in the experimental and control groups, respectively.

Two sets of research instruments were utilized:

1. an Intake, Periodic, and Discharge Questionnaire, developed by the research staff of the health department, which was utilized primarily for an assessment of participants' qualification for the CCL program as well as for a continuing assessment of such problematic areas as physical, social, emotional, and medical well-being, and activities of daily living,

2. a package of six research instruments compiled and edited by the research staff at the Levindale Geriatric Research Center, which was utilized primarily for the pretests and posttests of the participants' functional levels, including their level of satisfaction with later life.

Some interesting information was generated from this study. The CCL participants were able to improve or maintain their conditions of physical and mental health and the capability of self-maintenance compared to the control group participants. In addition, CCL participants indicated a higher level of satisfaction with their later life compared to the control group participants, although data showed no difference between the two groups with respect to reestablishment of life styles.

Furthermore, during the study period, two participants in the control group were admitted to nursing homes, while none of the CCL participants were. However, two CCL participants were institutionalized: one was admitted to a tuberculosis hospital and another entered an acute care hospital for surgery. Data showed an improvement made by participants of both groups in interpersonal relationships.

It should be noted that in the area of participants' independence in the activities of daily living, a greater percentage of control group participants demonstrated improvement. Sixty-six percent of the control group participants became more independent in their activities of daily living, while only 36 percent of the CCL participants became more independent. This conclusion is based on 10 items relating to subject's behavior in specific activities. The difference between the CCL and community groups were found statistically significant at the .05 level. These results were contradicted by another measure of behavioral independence utilized in the study, which showed that 60 percent of the CCL respondents improved in behavioral independence compared to 7 percent of the community group.

The per diem cost of the CCL program was computed based on the total program costs, which included personnel, space rental, and equipment costs. Additionally, the participants' out-of-pocket expense incurred outside CCL was computed to make a per diem comparison among related services (see appendix C). Results indicated that the CCL program cost was $12.99 a day for each participant, and the out-of-pocket expense was estimated at $3.98 a day for each participant. Adding both costs, it was estimated that the total CCL program would cost approximately $16.97 to sustain a participant at home with the day care service.

The most expensive program of the center was the provision of meals. Analysis revealed that meals were costing $4.22 per participant per day. This cost reflects the purchase of meals from a local catering service at $1.25 per person and over $6,000 worth of personnel time. The next most costly program was health services. Most expenses are incurred in this category by contractual services and nursing staff. Recreation ranks as the third most expensive program and transportation as the least costly component of the center.

Since adult day care is an experimental service in the United States, it was decided to make an estimate of what it would cost to start a new day care center. From the analysis of initial expenditures, it was learned that approximately $61,300 would be needed to cover start-up costs and eight months of operation. This includes the initial capital expenditures of approximately $13,400 for two vans, furniture, and medical equipment. Therefore, projecting this for a full year of operation, a total of $72,000 is needed. This figure includes the number and type of staff described in this study, renting 4,000 square feet of space at $3.00 per square foot, and a participant capacity of about 30.

It is concluded, therefore, that the adult day care center could be justifiably effective and a less costly alternative program to the present system of long-term care for chronically ill elderly patients. The data for the CCL evaluation are still being collected and analyzed for further documentation.

Mosholu-Montefiore's Research and Evaluation Activities

The Montefiore program, located in the northwest Bronx, New York City, has been in operation since the summer of 1972. The program has been affiliated with the Mosholu-Montefiore Community Center (MMCC) and the Associated YM-YWHAs of Greater New York. The goals of the program are:

1. to show that program participation will reduce the incidence of long-term institutionalization,

2. to show that program participation will be accompanied by improved health status and morale,

3. to develop a new model for the reimbursement of such services in a free-standing facility through adaptation of existing state Medicaid regulations,

4. to determine whether or not the provision of such service is cost effective when compared with the cost of long-term institutional care.

To identify the degree of goal accomplishment and cost effectiveness, an evaluative study was conducted by Community Research Applications, Inc., of New York, for approximately a two-year period (spring, 1973, through March, 1975), under a grant from Title IV of the Older Americans Act.[12] The study used an experimental research design that had one experimental group and two closely matched control groups and that involved pretests and posttests 18 months apart. All subjects in the experimental group were participants of the day care program selected from the patients referred to the Montefiore Day Care program by MMCC, Jewish Association for Services to the Aged (JASA), Montefiore Hospital, other community agencies, and private physicians. Twelve subjects were selected as control group one from people who were referred but not accepted for the day care program, and 33 were selected as control group two from the JASA case records. The research staff developed a third control group of 22 elderly patients who were discharged from the day care program. However, the third control group was used for descriptive rather than comparative purposes.

The Montefiore evaluative study used two published research instruments: the Illinois Form, which consists of 18 different scales that assess the health status of the participants, and the Life Satisfaction Index developed by Neugarten et al.[13] A third instrument used for this study was a daily log, recorded every eighth week and based on staff observation and participant activities. Dimensions along which observations of patients were recorded in the daily log included the following: participation in group education, participation in group discussion and counseling, participation in group exercise, participation in group recreation, participation in individual recreation, activity with community center group, participation in individual crafts (A.M. and P.M.), interaction with other members (A.M. and P.M.), and interaction with staff members (A.M. and P.M.).

The study found that while 13 percent of the experimental group participants were institutionalized, 33 percent of both control groups one and two were institutionalized during the study period. This differential effect was statistically significant. Although control group three was not developed for a comparison, it is interesting to note that 23 percent of the participants in this group were institutionalized. Based on these data, it was concluded that the day care program significantly reduced the rate of institutionalization for the group and delayed the onset of institutionalization for some individuals. However, the day care participants' health status was not significantly affected by the day care program and was maintained without any marked deterioration. Also, this study found there were no significant differences in life satisfaction between experimental and control groups over time.

The per diem cost of the day care service was computed, based on the total program costs ($34.80), plus in-kind services provided by the YM-YWHAs ($3.05), and luncheon costs ($1.50), for a total cost of $39.35 per person per day. On an annual basis, day care costs were estimated at between $6,500 and $7,000 per person; the cost for skilled nursing home and for intermediate care facility services in the same locale was $15,000 and $6,300, respectively.

The study recommended that day care programs be offered as new types of health services to elderly patients, that a differential and rational assignment of patients to the service facilities be effected, and that a further determination of the benefits associated with various health services be made.

On Lok's Research and Evaluation Activities

The final report of the On Lok project was prepared in September, 1975, as part of a demonstration project under a contract with the Chinatown, San Francisco-North Beach Health Care Planning and Development Corporation, which established service programs at On Lok Senior Health Services. The study evaluated the On Lok program in terms of the participants' mental and physical capacities, the participants' service satisfaction, and the per diem cost of the program.[14]

The study design was characterized by the development of closely matched experimental and control groups and by the administration of pretests and posttests. The sample consisted of a randomly selected experimental group of 4 patients in skilled nursing homes and another 11 patients in intermediate care facilities. They were placed in the day care center. The control group consisted of 12 patients from intermediate care and 3 patients from skilled nursing facilities. Research instruments such as the Patient Satisfaction Questionnaire and Functional Capacity and Mental Conditions Symptoms Scales were utilized for pretests and posttests in the five-month study period.

The study concluded that On Lok participants showed significantly greater satisfaction than did control group participants, and their satisfaction had increased during the study. The measurement of change in On Lok participants' functional capacity and mental conditions was inconclusive. Nevertheless, data indicated that On Lok participants were able to function in their community with no adverse consequences as long as On Lok services were available. For the On Lok group and the control group originally selected from the intermediate care facility patients, the costs were $17.21 and $19.98, respectively, per day per participant; for the groups of skilled nursing home patients, the costs were $21.03 and $21.47, respectively. Thus, the On Lok program was proved to be less costly by 14 percent and 2 percent for the participants from intermediate care facilities and skilled nursing homes, respectively, and in total, the cost saving by On Lok was 8 percent.

Major recommendations were to continue the demonstration project and to establish the following evaluation criteria: evaluation by an independent agency, the development of a specific evaluation instrument, redefinition of "maintenance" as well as "change," the inclusion of a variety of control group participants who live at home with assistance through home health services, and the development of a better method of collecting fiscal data.

Demonstration and Evaluation of Long-Term Care in Section 222(b) Projects

Under P. L. 92–603, Section 222 (b), contracts for research and demonstration projects were granted to six different service agencies through the Division of Health Service Evaluation, DHEW, effective July, 1974, to determine the suitability of day care services and homemaker services as expanded benefits under Medicare and Medicaid. Demonstration grants were awarded to the following six agencies:

1. for demonstration of homemaker services only: Inter-City Home Health Association, Los Angeles, California; and Homemaker-Home Health Aid Services of Rhode Island, in Providence.

2. for demonstrations of day care services only: Burke Rehabilitation Center, White Plains, New York; and St. Camillus Skilled Nursing Facility, Syracuse, New York,

3. for the demonstration of both homemaker and day care services: San Francisco Home Health Agency, San Francisco, California; and Lexington-Fayette County Health Department, Lexington, Kentucky.

An additional demonstration grant was awarded to the Albert Einstein College of Medicine, the Bronx, New York, through the Division of Health Systems Design and Development, DHEW, to evaluate its experimental program, Day Hospital Service.

All projects except Day Hospital Service were required to follow and utilize research designs, procedures, and protocols developed by Medicus Systems Corporation (MSC), Chicago, Illinois, which was awarded a contract to perform the evaluation of the demonstration programs. Data were to be collected by research staff at each demonstration project, and the raw data were to be forwarded to and analyzed by MSC. The evaluation instrument included the following items: social and demographic status, mental-physical functioning, activities of daily living, social-psychological status, Raven Test (a test for respondents' decision-making capacity), and medical impairment. Each project had expanded benefits (experimental) and control groups consisting of 50 or more subjects screened by the assessment team (physician, nurse, and social worker) for each group. The control group was determined by randomizing patients accepted into the project who qualified for either expanded benefit (day care or homemaker services). Those patients randomized into the control group did not receive the expanded Medicare or Medicaid benefits. The experimental group received the expanded benefit coverage (whether or not they actually use the service was part of the information gathered). All project subjects were reassessed every 3 months during a 12-month period.

It was anticipated that these projects would be completed in early 1977 and the research findings presented to the United States Congress for consideration in the expansion of the present system of Medicaid and Medicare benefits.[15]

Conclusion

The evaluation aspects of most day care centers are closely integrated with the clinical and administrative aspects of program operations. Whatever the evaluation approach is, the most difficult parameters to deal with are adequate controls and accurate costs for all support systems involved. Two of the major pitfalls of many research efforts are "data poisoning" (i.e., collecting too much data to analyze properly, which results in inadequate analyses and interpretations) and too few study participants to test adequately for statistical significance.

Each day care center and therefore each evaluation has many unique features. Collectively, however, these studies offer answers to many of the broad policy questions that have served as barriers to the expansion of noninstitutional long-term care services throughout the United States. Few delivery systems have been so extensively studied before implementation into a national policy as adult day care.

Notes

1. H. Grauer and F. Birenbaum, "A Geriatric Functional Rating Scale to Determine the Need for Institutional Care," *Journal of the American Geriatric Society,* vol. 23, no. 10, 1975, pp. 472–476; Lee Gurel, Margaret Linn, and Bernard F. Linn, "Physical and Mental Impairment of Function Evaluation in the Aged: The PAMIE Scale," *Journal of Gerontology,* vol. 27, no. 1, 1972, pp. 83–90; Ellen W. Jones, with assistance from Barbara J. McWitt and Eleanor McKnight, *Patient Classification for Long-Term Care: User's Manual* (Washington, D.C.: Department of Health, Education and Welfare, Publication No. HRA–74–3107, December 1973); Sidney Katz et al., *Effects of Continued Care: A Study of Chronic Illness in the Home* (Washington, D.C.: Department of Health, Education and Welfare, Publication No. HSM–73–3010, 1972); Sidney Katz et al., "Progress in the Development of the Index of ADL," *The Gerontologist,* part 1, Spring 1970, pp. 20–30; Sidney Katz et al., "Study of Illness in the Aged; The Index of ADL: A Standardized Measure of Biological and Psychological Functioning," *Journal of the American Medical Association,* vol. 185, 1963, pp. 914–929; M. Powell Lawton, *Assessing the Competence of Older People* (New York: Behavior Publications, Inc., Research and Planning Action for the Elderly, 1972), pp. 122–142; M. Powell Lawton, "The Functional Assessment of Elderly People," *Journal of the American Geriatric Society,* vol. 19, no. 6, 1971, pp. 465–481; Richard Nauen, Martin Weitzner, and Jones N. Muller, "A Method for Planning for Care of Long-Term Patients," *American Journal of Public Health,* vol. 58, 1968, pp. 2111–2119; Bernice Neugarten, Robert Havighurst, and Sheldon Tobin, "Measurement of Life Satisfaction," *Journal of Gerontology,* vol. 16, no. 2, 1961, pp. 134–143; Sylvia Sherwood, John N. Morris, and Esther Barnhard, "Developing a System for Assigning Individuals into an Appropriate Residential Setting," *Journal of Gerontology,* vol. 30, no. 3, 1975, pp. 331–342.

2. *Request for Proposal No. HRA–106–HFR–234 (4)*, for Experiments and Demonstrations Authorized under Public Law 92–603, Section 222(b), for Intermediate Care Facilities, Homemaker Service and Day Care Services (Rockville, Md.: Health Resources Administration, Public Health Service, Department Health, Education and Welfare, April 12, 1974).

3. *Triage: Coordinated Services to the Elderly* (Hartford, Conn.: The Connecticut State Department on Aging, 1976).

4. Marie E. Micknick, L. Jeff Harris, Richard A. Willis, and Jamesina E. Williams, *Ambulatory Care Evaluation: A Primer for Quality Review* (Los Angeles, Calif.: Regents of the University of California, 1976).

5. Hubert M. Blalock, *Causal Inferences in Nonexperimental Research* (Chapel Hill, N.C.: University of North Carolina Press, 1961); Hubert M. Blalock, *Causal Models in the Social Sciences* (Chicago, Ill.: Aldine-Atherton, 1971); Edgar F. Borgatta, ed., *Sociological Methodology* (San Francisco, Calif.: Jossey-Bass, Inc., 1969), chapters 1 and 2; Sewall Wright, "Correlation and Causation," *Journal of Agricultural Research*, vol. 20, 1921, pp. 557–585; Sewall Wright "Path Coefficients and Path Regressions: Alternative or Complementary Concepts?" *Biometrics*, vol. 16, 1960, pp. 189–202; Sewall Wright, "The Method of Path Coefficients, *Annals of Mathematical Statistics*, vol. 5, 1934, pp. 161–215. All of these references are useful for knowledge on causal pattern analysis.

6. "Guidelines for Geriatric Day Hospitals," F/G, 54/17 (London, England: Department of Health and Social Security, December 7, 1971).

7. Eric Pfeiffer, "Multidimensional Quantitative Assessment of Three Populations of Elderly," paper presented at the 27th Annual Meeting of the Gerontological Society, Miami Beach, Fla., Nov. 5–9, 1973; E. Shanas, "Health Status of Older People: Cross-National Implications," *American Journal of Public Health*, vol. 64, no. 3, 1974, pp. 261–264.

8. Eloise Rathbone-McCuan, *An Evaluation of a Geriatric Day Care Center as a Parallel Service to Institutional Care* (Baltimore, Md.: Levindale Geriatric Research Center, 1973).

9. Eloise Rathbone-McCuan, Harold Lohn, Julia Levenson, and James Hou, *Cost-Effectiveness Evaluation of the Levindale Adult*

Day Treatment Center (Baltimore Md.: Levindale Geriatric Center, 1975).

10. Ibid.

11. Philip G. Weiler, Paul K. H. Kim, and Larry Pickard, "Health Care for Elderly Americans: Evaluation of an Adult Day Health Care Model," *Medical Care,* vol. 14, 1976, pp. 700–708.

12. Douglas Holmes and Edwin Hudson, *Evaluation Report of the Mosholu-Montefiore Day Care Center* (New York: Community Research Applications, Inc., 1975).

13. Bernice Neugarten, Robert Havighurst, and Sheldon Tobin, "Measurement of Life Satisfaction," *Journal of Gerontology,* vol. 16, no. 2, 1961, pp. 134–143.

14. *Evaluation Study of On Lok Senior Health Services Demonstration Project* (San Francisco, Calif.: California Department of Health, On Lok Senior Health Services, 1975).

15. *Long-Term Care Demonstrations and Experiments Manual* (Chicago, Ill.: Medicus Systems Corp., November 6, 1974; revised ed., March 6, 1975).

Useful Readings

Anderson, Nancy N., *A Planning Study of Services to Non-Institutionalized Older Persons in Minnesota* (Minneapolis, Minn.: Contract by Faculty and Staff of the School of Public Affairs, University of Minnesota, 1974).

Brickner, Philip W., and Janeski, J. F., *The Chelsea-Village Program: 3-Year Report* (New York: St. Vincent's Hospital, 1976).

Flathman, David P., and Donald E. Larsen, *Evaluation of Three Geriatric Day Hospitals in Alberta* (Edmonton, Alberta: The University of Alberta Medical School, 1976).

Peschke, Manfred, *Needs and Potential of Day Services in New Hampshire* (Concord, N.H.: Senior Enrichment Services, 1975).

Weissert, William G., "Costs of Adult Day Care: A Comparison to Nursing Homes," *Inquiry* (to be published).

12

Directions for the Future

Summary

In this book we have attempted to synthesize the experiences of a select group of practitioners, administrators, and researchers who have individual and collective experience with the delivery of geriatric day care services. These services have been discussed within a framework that emphasizes the interrelationship between the health and social components of long-term care. Day care services have been considered from the standpoint of caring for the chronically ill patient, who may experience acute episodes but differs radically from the younger acute patient in his or her need for comprehensive care that is not under the aegis of a single health practitioner.

The model of long-term care described stresses interdisciplinary care, multiagency-based service, access routes simple enough for the elderly person to manipulate, and services flexible and permanent enough for the elderly person's utilization pattern. The person's need and service preference are posed as the necessary triggering mechanisms for obtaining service supports when and where intervention is required. Society must begin moving toward the establishment of such care continuums to meet the ever-growing needs of the older segment of the population.

Developmental Generalizations

The data now available provide some basis for limited generalization about the development patterns of day care centers:

Usually, there is one person committed to the idea of day care. This person assumes the major responsibility for becoming knowledgeable about the concept, developing the original plan, and introducing the concept within the agency and to the broader community.

The promoting person meets with enthusiasm when the concept is presented, but many roadblocks arise in implementing the concept, not the least of which is obtaining the funds required to start the program and planning for the ongoing funding base of the center. Centers funded by a preliminary grant from the federal, state, or local government are able to move rapidly into program development.

The type of person (i.e., the level and pattern of impairment) identified for the target population tends to be determined by the scope of the resources available to the day care center. Initially, it is conceived as a service for persons whose needs fall in the service gap between the senior citizen center and institution. These people are too mentally and/or physically impaired to attend a senior citizen center profitably, yet do not require 24-hour institutionalization.

Determining the combination of health and social services to be introduced and setting service priorities is an almost universal problem. Typically, there is a clear recognition that the aged to be served in these centers require a comprehensive set of supportive social services, but the potential third-party reimbursement sources require an emphasis on health services.

Two day care centers have been described in detail. The service delivery experiences of these centers were used as fundamental data sources that enabled the authors to generalize from two programs to many. Day care centers can and should be developed and administered by a range of service agencies. The Lexington-Fayette County Health Department represents a sponsoring organization with service orientation and mandate different from that of the Levindale Hebrew Geriatric Center and Hospital.

Chapters 5, 6, 7, and 8 deal with specific dimensions of health and social service delivery within day care centers, emphasizing basic principles of professional care. Standards of quality care should not be compromised when services are provided to elderly patients, but methodologies and professional roles are and should often be modified to complement the needs of the elderly.

In planning the range of therapies to be provided in any center, a balance must be struck among the level of participant need, projected costs, and the possible alternative methods available for providing these services to individuals. Clustering the maximum number of therapies in a day care center is justifiable only by the needs of participants. Different types of geriatric day care will require different forms and ranges of therapeutic rehabilitation services.

The buttressing factor for all effective day care center operations is an administrative structure that can provide the necessary management and organizational leadership. The sponsoring organization as well as the day care center program must exhibit administrative leadership. These two levels of administrative leadership are not necessarily filled by the same individuals. Different patterns of administrative leadership are described for the Lexington and Levindale centers, and there are an infinite number of patterns that can be incorporated into day care center operations.

Policy Implications

Geriatric day care is a new direction in aging. Day care is the focus for needed changes in the policy toward long-term care in this country. It is as much a spirit of rejuvenation in the field of aging as it is a new type of service; focusing on this new care has captured and renewed the interest of diverse professionals in the field. It has forced us to rethink our policies toward long-term care and the potential of a meaningful life for the infirmed aged. Through day care we are heading away from isolation and the prejudices of "agism."[1] We are beginning to move toward integration of the services for and needs of older people.

Merteus[2] has discussed the role of technology in change. Technology usually has dictated changes in the way services are delivered;

this is exemplified by the changes in services in the modern hospital. Day care, on the other hand, was stimulated not by any change in technology but by a change in perception. There was a need to do more than what was being done and a need and value for doing it differently.

In pointing to a new direction, day care should lead away from the mistakes in the development of nursing homes. The pitfalls that should be avoided are:

1. Before a national reimbursement mechanism is set up through third-party payers, a satisfactory system of day care centers must be established. If not, the monetary stimulus may:

   a. cause an inflationary spiral for day care services by increasing demand faster than supply,

   b. cause a boom and bust cycle (many inferior day centers will be established to siphon off the new flood of cash; then, as costs soar and there are cutbacks, a rash of closures will result, having a devastating effect on services),

   c. cause quality to suffer because of the pressure to provide services and keep up with demand,

   d. cause overutilization or inappropriate utilization.

2. Day care centers should not be developed in a vacuum, isolated from the rest of the social and health care delivery system. When this happens quality always suffers. All too often, nursing homes have not been part of a system but only dead ends. To avoid this, the new direction points to the following areas:

   a. Day centers should be an integral part of another system providing either health or social services (e.g., hospitals, health departments, educational centers, social agencies, health maintenance organizations, group practices).

   b. Day centers should be integrated into the educational model for professionals in the field of human services. Students should participate actively in their training in various settings for the delivery of care for the aged.

3. There has been overreliance on the physician to correct all the deficiencies in nursing homes. While the physician's participation is critical even in day care centers, it is only part of the effort. Many other professionals are involved and must share the responsibility. Society has, in the past, given moral and legal sanction to practice the

healing arts to the physician, who has taken this responsibility seriously and tended to view it globally. Thus, a value system developed that is now cumbersome and outdated. In day care, with portions of patient care delegated to others, the concept of final medical responsibility is no longer appropriate. The use of nurse practitioners and physician assistants has been stimulated as a result of this new trend. Day care has emphasized the need for team or shared responsibility. The physician in this age of specialization cannot possibly meet all the needs implied in a continuum of care. Therefore, to insist on this is only to insure the failure of the system.

4. The temptation to overstandardize must be avoided. Standards will not cure all the ills in the system and can stifle initiative, prevent flexibility to meet local needs, and increase cost without improving care. Day care centers have not been able to fit into a definite model; standards will have to be flexible. The tendency to clarify, label, and categorize both day care centers and their patients can be counterproductive. Centers should vary according to local need and the patient mix should vary; these are probably important components of success.

5. In addition, the issue of proprietary vs. nonprofit centers must be addressed. If proprietary institutions were profit maximizers and nonprofit institutions were quality maximizers, the answer would be simple. However, this is not always the case. If reimbursement could be related to quality, the issue of proprietary vs. nonprofit would be irrelevant.

6. A new approach to financing long-term care must be established that addresses both the medical and nonmedical aspects of the wide range of human need. Such an approach could separate room and board costs from medical and other service costs. Social and medical services could be provided and reimbursed in a flexible fashion to support people in any setting (institution, congregate living arrangement, private home, the person's own home, adult day care). Separating room and board from service costs permits a much simpler and more efficient utilization of financing for supporting people. It also gets us out of the morass of facility definitions. Levels of care would be tied solely to an individual and not to an institution, making it possible to provide for a continuum of care tailored to individual need.

This does not lock us into a medical model that has a built-in tendency for fiscal escalation because of personnel restrictions and technological demands.

7. Ideally, day care centers will not face the difficulties of nursing homes in recruiting competent professional staff, because training centers for health care professionals are building geriatrics and gerontology into educational and training formats. The challenges of working in a day care center are many. Provision of services, attitudes, and the approach to the participant all make a difference in treatment outcomes. In an effective day care center there is no room for staff members who cling to the perceptions and attitudes that sustain the myths of "tragedy" and "irreversible conditions." A center is a place of opportunity for the participant. The staff becomes the most vital factor in making that opportunity a reality.

Furthermore, day care centers are set up to be as stimulating to the staff as to the participants; total emphasis on either is destructive to the program. To accomplish this, attention is paid to the patient mix (as discussed on chapter 6), which provides the staff with some success and the participants with role models of success; center activities are enjoyed by staff and patients alike and are therapeutic to both.

Some reasons why day care occupies its present role and has met with success are:

1. The service environment is structured to emphasize function and not diagnoses. One has only to walk into a thriving day care program to see the excitement of the frail and impaired aged as they participate: "My health problems are risky. I never thought I'd be so sick and still live at home. Coming here gives me a lot of reassurance, but I don't think you make me feel helpless. I felt that way when I was staying at home last year."

Day care stimulates capacities for independence while at the same time providing supports for functional limitations. The nursing home experience has shown that it is as untherapeutic to overservice as to underservice the aged patient. A successful day care center strikes the balance so often absent in institutional settings.

2. Patients need to be prepared to manage through evenings and weekends. This makes it necessary for the staff to have a very specific time frame to work in to get everything done. It also gives

them an objective each day. This differs drastically from the situation in nursing homes, where problems can get passed from one shift to the other.

3. Many visitors, family members, volunteers, and students come to the centers. This constant exposure to new and interested people can act as a very good stimulus for quality control because there is continual incentive for staff to make things presentable, problems cannot be sequestered from the public view, less involved people are more outspoken about any deficiencies they may find, the public relations that develop stimulate community involvement and interest. It has been suggested that this approach also be used in nursing homes to improve quality of care.[3]

4. Patients can more readily report back to family and friends about their care at the center. This also can be a method of quality control.

5. The day care center falls into the patient's routine of life. To spend the day in a setting different from the home and return to the familiar surroundings of the home in the evenings is rarely disturbing since it is similar in many respects to normal previous experience.

Rapid emergence of day care facilities should be viewed with cautious optimism. There are dangers in expecting too much from "fashionable" programs. For professionals newly involved with a program or just acquainting themselves with the concept, there is the tendency to evaluate its merits only optimistically. It is not uncommon to hear a new convert strongly defending day care as being more therapeutic than home care or sheltered housing, even to the point of giving day care development total priority.

This approach would be hazardous if taken seriously by policy makers and planners. Day care cannot substitute for intensive care and professional monitoring on a 24-hour basis. It cannot be considered an option for an aged person who refuses to join a group setting in order to receive rehabilitation and socialization services. To assume that day care is the final solution and to stimulate the growth only of day care centers is to thwart the development of a viable long-term care system.

While many evaluation programs are underway and much discussion is taking place, their outcome will probably relate to how, and not if, day care centers should develop nationally and to what effects this will have on care for the elderly. Nothing is so powerful as an idea whose time has come. Day care in this country is such an idea.

Notes

1. Robert N. Butler, *Why Survive? Being Old in America* (New York: Harper and Row, 1975).

2. Charles Merteus, "Introducing Social Change in a New Industrial Society," *Modern Government*, vol. 8, October 1969, pp. 68–72.

3. Sharon Winn and Kenneth McCoffree, "Characteristics of Nursing Homes Perceived to Be Effective and Efficient," paper presented at the 28th Annual Scientific Meeting of the Gerontological Society, Louisville, Ky., October 26, 1975.

Appendix A
Intake, Periodic,
and Discharge Questionnaire

Interviewee(s)_____ Date Completed _____

_____ Interviewer_____

NAME_____
     Last   First   Middle

ADDRESS_____
     Number   Street   City   State

Telephone Number _____ Former Occupation _____

Religion_____

Birthdate_____ Age _____ Race _____

Family Structure (List Significant Relatives in the Client's Life)

Name	Address	Relationship	Phone Number

Hospital Preference _____

Physician_____

Dentist _____

Optometrist/Ophthalmologist _____

Podiatrist_____

Referred by_____ Phone Number_____

Reasons for Referral_____

Client Desires to Attend CCL   Yes _____   No_____

Source of Payment: Medicare_____ Number_____Eff. Date_____

                   Medicaid_____ Number_____

                   Title XX_____ Private Pay_____

                   No Pay _____ Other _____

Soc. Security #_____ Income_____ IPDQ Score_____

Appendix A

A. MEDICAL

	YES	NO
Does the client have any of the following illnesses for which he/she is <u>receiving treatment</u>?		
1. Diabetes		
2. Hypertension		
3. Coronary Artery Disease		
4. Cerebral Vascular Disease		
5. Peripheral Vascular Disease		
6. Chronic Bronchitis		
7. Emphysema		
8. Asthma		
9. Arthritis		
10. Peptic Ulcer		
11. Hiatus Hernia		
12. Cancer		
13. Cirrhosis		
14. Thyroid Hyper Hypo (circle)		
15. Glaucoma		
16. Cataracts		
17. Prostate		
18. Parkinsonism		
19. Kidney Disease		
20. Congestive Heart Failure		
21. Psychiatric Diseases Type:		
22. Other		
23. Have you been hospitalized in the past year?		
24. Do you eat just because you think you should?		

	YES	NO

25. Do you have a hearing problem?

26. Do you have a sight problem?
    (a) Are you able to watch TV?

27. Do you have trouble breathing?

28. Are you on a special diet?

29. Are you taking a prescribed medication?
    If so, please list all medications:

    _____   _____

    _____   _____

    _____   _____

30. If so, does someone give you your medicine?

31. Do you have problems controlling your bladder?

32. Do you have problems controlling your bowels?

33. Do you have painful corns, bunions, etc.?

B. ACTIVITIES OF DAILY LIVING

34. Do you need help when you bathe?

35. Do you need help dressing?

36. Do you need assistance in cleaning your
    teeth or dentures?

37. Are you unable to do your grocery shopping?

38. Are you unable to prepare your own meals?

39. Do you need help to eat?

40. Does someone help you use the telephone?

41. Do you have difficulty in writing with a
    pen or pencil?

42. Are you unable to clean the house?

43. Are you unable to wash the dishes?

Appendix A

	YES	NO

C. PHYSICAL

44. ·Do you need assistance in getting in or out of bed?

45. Do you need assistance in sitting down or getting up from a chair?

46. Do you need assistance in using the toilet?

47. Do you need the assistance of crutches, cane, walker, wheelchair or other appliance? (circle the appliance used)

48. Do you have problems walking up and down the stairs?

49. Do you have difficulty opening or closing doors?

50. Do you have difficulty turning knobs?

51. Do you have difficulty picking up objects over 5 pounds off the floor?

52. Have you fallen in the past year?

53. Do you have disabilities which limit the use of your upper extremities?
Specify:_____

_____

54. Do you have disabilities which limit the use of your lower extremities?
Specify:_____

_____

To what extent have these disabilities impaired the use of fine motor skills? Specify:

_____

_____

_____

166

	YES	NO

D. EMOTIONAL

55. Are you more forgetful now than you used to be?

56. Do you have frequent periods when you feel
     restless or angry?
     (a) What things make you feel that way?

     _____

     _____

     _____

57. Do you often have periods when you feel sad?
     (a) What makes you feel sad?

     _____

     _____

     _____

58. Do you have problems getting other people to
     understand you?

59. Do you get lost easily?

60. Do you often lose your personal belongings?

61. Have you lost a close friend or relative within
     the past year?
     (a) If yes, how has this affected you?

     _____

     _____

     _____

62. Have you ever been hospitalized for a
     psychiatric illness?

     How many times?_____

     Give dates_____

     _____

     Reason(s) for Admission_____

     _____

Appendix A

	YES	NO

E. SOCIAL

63. Do you have problems getting along with your family?

    (a) If yes, specify_____

    _____

64. Do you have trouble getting along with your neighbors?

65. Are you unable to visit your friends regularly?

66. Are your family members unable to be out of your house for employment or other purposes?

67. Are you unable to attend church or other social activities?

68. Are you unable to make friends easily?

69. Do you have frequent arguments with your friends or family?

70. Do you live alone?

71. If so, is your family unable to visit regularly?

(Note: Code Items 72-75 as follows: Yes=0, No=1)

72. Do you have a favorite pastime or hobby?
    (a) If yes, specify:_____

    _____

    _____

73. Do you like to be involved in community projects?

74. Do you like to be involved in arts and crafts?

75. Can you play a musical instrument or are you interested in music to any degree?

	YES	NO

F. INTERVIEWER'S EVALUATION

From your observations, does the client have any of the following problems?

76. Personal hygiene poor?

77. Disorientation to time, place and person?

78. Withdrawn?

79. Uncooperative?

80. Belligerent and hostile?

81. Over talkative?

82. Bizarre mannerisms?

83. Appears undernourished?

84. Careless smoker?

85. Poor family interaction?

86. Other?

87. Poor living environment?

88. Comments:

G. (a) How can the applicant benefit from the Centers' services?

_____

_____

(b) Are there anticipated adjustments/ problems when the applicant begins attending the Center? If yes, please specify_____

_____

_____

(c) Why does the applicant (and family) want to attend the Center for Creative Living?_____

_____

Appendix B
Utilization/Review
Evaluation Summary

Patient_____

1. (a) Was Admission Appropriate?   ___Yes   ___No
   (b) Is Continuation Appropriate?   ___Yes   ___No

2. Service Utilization:

Services	Provided	Goals Short-Term Set?	Long-Term Set?	Goals Met?	Service Need to Continue
Skilled Nursing					
Personal Care					
Nutrition					
Physical Therapy					
Speech Therapy					
Recreational Therapy					
Social Work					
Occupational Therapy					
Opthalmology					
Podiatry					
Dental					
Routine Screening					
Other					
Other					

3. Recommendations: 4. Comments:

_____(a) Continue at present prescribed rate.

_____(b) Reduce rate to____days per week.

_____(c) Discharge

Appendix C

Per Diem Cost of Living Data Sheet

1. If_____(he/she/you) live alone
   or with spouse, what is monthly rent
   and utilities cost?

   answer_____ = _____(1a)
                      30

   or if own onw home what is monthly
   house payment if there is any?

   answer_____ = _____(1b)
                      30

   check here if own home outright____
   if this is true, what is utility
   rate per month?

   answer_____ = _____(1c)
                      30

2. How many visits to your doctor
   or clinic have you made in the
   past 12 months?

   answer_____ = _____ = _____(2)
              12   30

3. How many visits have/has____(he/she/you)
   made to the following in the past 12
   months other than at the Center for
   Creative Living?

a.	dentist	_____
b.	eye doctor	_____
c.	podiatrist	_____
d.	psychiatrist	_____
e.	other	_____

dentist	x a =	_____
eye doctor	x b =	_____
poliatrist	x c =	_____
psychiatrist	x d =	_____
other	x e =	_____

   total   _____ = _____ = _____(3)
                     12   30

4. Have (you/he/she) had any hospitalization in the last 12 months?

   how many days = _____ x = _____ = _____(4)
                                      90

Appendix C

5. Any special treatment during those
   visits - if so what were total
   costs?

   answer_____ =   _____(5)
                    90

6. Any emergency room use? How many
   times in the last 12 months?

   answer_____ x = _____ = ____ =   _____ _____(6)
                                    12   30

7. Total costs for special treatment
   while in emergency room.

   answer_____ =   _____(7)
                    90

8. Total cost of any lab work in
   the past 12 months.

   answer_____ = _____ =   _____(8)
                    12   30

9. What is the average number of bus
   trips per week?

   answer_____ x = _____ =   _____(9)
                                     7

   number of cab trips per week

   answer_____ x = _____ =   _____(10)
                                     7

   Average number of miles driven
   in car per week

   answer_____ x = _____ =   _____(11)
                                     7

10. What do you estimate (you/his/her)
    food cost per week?

    answer_____ =   _____(12)
                     7

11. What are (you/his/her) estimated
    total clothing costs in the
    past 12 months?

    answer_____ = _____ =   _____(13)
                     12   30

12. What do you estimate (your/his/her)
    monthly entertainment costs to be?
    (excluding any major expenditures)

    answer_____ =   _____(14)
                     30

    any major expenditures: what_____
                             total cost_____   _____(14)

13. Other weekly expenses?

answer_____ =   _____(15)
            7

14. Do you use paid help at home?
If so, how many times per week
and how much?

answer_____ x _____ =   _____(16)
                        7

15. What do you estimate your total
medication costs per month to be?
(include both prescription and
patent medicines)

answer_____ =   _____(17)

16. Have you purchased or rented any of
the following in the last 12 months?

                              Cost or rent/month

wheel chair   _____
hearing aid   _____
speech aid   _____
prothesis   _____
walker   _____
other   _____

        total   _____ = _____(18)
                          30

17. Do you use any other community
services - if so what?   _____(19)

18. Do you think there are any other
expenses in the past 12 months
that have not been covered?

answer in total dollars_____ = _____ =   _____(19)
                    30   12

Appendix D
Community Resource Agencies

Resource agencies that may be supportive in collaboration with day care services are (the list is not exhaustive but contains representative sources of assistance for day care centers):

1. Medical/Social Service Groups

Type of support: services

Local Hospitals
Mental Health Centers
Health Departments
Health Maintenance Organizations
Neighborhood Health Centers
Nursing Homes
Visiting Nurses Association/Home Health Agencies
City/County Welfare Departments
Professional Societies/Organizations: Dental, Medical, Pharmacy, Nursing, Hospital
Information and Referral Agency
Title VII Nutrition Centers
Meals-On-Wheels
Multipurpose Senior Citizens Centers
Friendly Visitor Service
Telephone Reassurance Service
Legal Aid Agency
Sheltered Workshops (vocational rehabilitation)
Senior Housing Programs
Group Apartments

2. Voluntary Groups

Type of support: personnel/services/funding

United Way/Community Chest
American Cancer Society
Red Cross
American Public Health Association
Local Councils on Aging
Clubs:
    Federated Women's Club
    Junior League
    Altrusa Club
    Rotary
    Kiwanis Club
    Lions Club
Neighborhood Organizations
Retired Senior Volunteer Program (RSVP)
Service Corps of Retired Executives (SCORE)
Volunteers in Service to America (VISTA)

3. Religious Groups

Type of support: facilities/funding

All Denominations

4. Educational Organizations

Type of support: services/consultation

Community Colleges (physical education departments)
Universities
Vocational Schools
Public Libraries

5. Planning Agencies

Type of support: consultation for funding and resource development

Health Systems Agencies
Economic Development Administration Agencies

6. Foundations

Type of support: funding

See *The Foundation Directory,* published by the Foundation Center (New York: Columbia University Press, July 1975).

7. Government Agencies

Type of support: facilities/services/funding

Department of Transportation (local/state)
Department of Parks and Recreation (local/state)
Department of Welfare (local/state)
Department of Social Services (local/state)
Commission on Aging (local/state)
Area Agencies on Aging (local/state)
U. S. Department of Health, Education and Welfare (federal)
   Health Resources Administration
   Social and Rehabilitative Services
   Social Security
   Administration on Aging
   Office for Human Development
U. S. Veterans Administration (federal)
U. S. Department of Commerce (community block grants)